INCENTIVES AND TEST-BASED ACCOUNTABILITY IN EDUCATION

I0720791

Committee on Incentives and Test-Based Accountability
in Public Education

Michael Hout and Stuart W. Elliott, *Editors*

Board on Testing and Assessment

Division of Behavioral and Social Sciences and Education

NATIONAL RESEARCH COUNCIL
OF THE NATIONAL ACADEMIES

THE NATIONAL ACADEMIES PRESS
Washington, D.C.
www.nap.edu

THE NATIONAL ACADEMIES PRESS   500 Fifth Street, N.W.   Washington, DC 20001

NOTICE: The project that is the subject of this report was approved by the Governing Board of the National Research Council, whose members are drawn from the councils of the National Academy of Sciences, the National Academy of Engineering, and the Institute of Medicine. The members of the committee responsible for the report were chosen for their special competences and with regard for appropriate balance.

This study was supported by Awards B7990 and D08025 from the Carnegie Corporation of New York, and Awards 2006-7514 and 2007-1580 from the William and Flora Hewlett Foundation. Additional funding was also provided by the Presidents' Committee of The National Academies. Any opinions, findings, conclusions, or recommendations expressed in this publication are those of the authors and do not necessarily reflect the views of the Carnegie Corporation of New York or the William and Flora Hewlett Foundation.

International Standard Book Number-13: 978-0-309-12814-8
International Standard Book Number-10: 0-309-12814-5

Additional copies of this report are available from the National Academies Press, 500 Fifth Street, N.W., Lockbox 285, Washington, DC 20055; (800) 624-6242 or (202) 334-3313 (in the Washington metropolitan area); Internet, http://www.nap.edu

Suggested citation: National Research Council. (2011). *Incentives and Test-Based Accountability in Education*. Committee on Incentives and Test-Based Accountability in Public Education, M. Hout and S.W. Elliott, *Editors*. Board on Testing and Assessment, Division of Behavioral and Social Sciences and Education. Washington, DC: The National Academies Press.

THE NATIONAL ACADEMIES
Advisers to the Nation on Science, Engineering, and Medicine

The **National Academy of Sciences** is a private, nonprofit, self-perpetuating society of distinguished scholars engaged in scientific and engineering research, dedicated to the furtherance of science and technology and to their use for the general welfare. Upon the authority of the charter granted to it by the Congress in 1863, the Academy has a mandate that requires it to advise the federal government on scientific and technical matters. Dr. Ralph J. Cicerone is president of the National Academy of Sciences.

The **National Academy of Engineering** was established in 1964, under the charter of the National Academy of Sciences, as a parallel organization of outstanding engineers. It is autonomous in its administration and in the selection of its members, sharing with the National Academy of Sciences the responsibility for advising the federal government. The National Academy of Engineering also sponsors engineering programs aimed at meeting national needs, encourages education and research, and recognizes the superior achievements of engineers. Dr. Charles M. Vest is president of the National Academy of Engineering.

The **Institute of Medicine** was established in 1970 by the National Academy of Sciences to secure the services of eminent members of appropriate professions in the examination of policy matters pertaining to the health of the public. The Institute acts under the responsibility given to the National Academy of Sciences by its congressional charter to be an adviser to the federal government and, upon its own initiative, to identify issues of medical care, research, and education. Dr. Harvey V. Fineberg is president of the Institute of Medicine.

The **National Research Council** was organized by the National Academy of Sciences in 1916 to associate the broad community of science and technology with the Academy's purposes of furthering knowledge and advising the federal government. Functioning in accordance with general policies determined by the Academy, the Council has become the principal operating agency of both the National Academy of Sciences and the National Academy of Engineering in providing services to the government, the public, and the scientific and engineering communities. The Council is administered jointly by both Academies and the Institute of Medicine. Dr. Ralph J. Cicerone and Dr. Charles M. Vest are chair and vice chair, respectively, of the National Research Council.

www.national-academies.org

Preface

This project originated in the Board on Testing and Assessment (BOTA) in 2002 as the No Child Left Behind (NCLB) Act of 2001 was in its early stages of implementation. The initial discussions were sparked by the different perspectives on the use of test-based incentives by the board members, whose expertise included a wide range of disciplines. In particular, the board's interest in the topic was animated by the apparent tension between the economics and educational measurement literatures about the potential of test-based accountability to improve student achievement.

As a result of its early discussions, BOTA held workshops about the use of incentives in 2003 and 2005. These early discussions were funded, in part, by support for BOTA from the U.S. Department of Education and the U.S. National Science Foundation. After these workshops the board identified, defined, and sought support for the research synthesis the board concluded could be undertaken. With generous funding from the Carnegie Corporation of New York and the William and Flora Hewlett Foundation, the Committee on Incentives and Test-Based Accountability in Public Education was appointed in early 2007 to carry on the work that BOTA had started.

The charge called for the committee to examine research related to the use of incentives and to synthesize its implications for the use of test-based incentives in education. The committee held three meetings, as well as a workshop on multiple measures and NCLB that was supported by additional funding from the Carnegie Corporation, the Hewlett Foundation, and the Presidents' Committee of The National Academies.

When work began on this topic 9 years ago, no one expected that the project would occupy most of a decade or that it would provide such an opportunity to survey a remarkable period of educational change. As the report notes in Chapter 1, the use of test-based incentives in education has been growing for several decades. However, it was in the first decade of the 21st century—which saw the enactment of NCLB, the maturation of the state movement for using high school exit exams, and the strong interest in using newly-available student test data to tie teacher pay to value-added analyses of their students' test results—that the use of test-based incentives truly took hold of the education policy world. At the same time, there has been a transformation in the rigor of the methods used to analyze educational data. The combination of policy experimentation and new research methods has produced the set of studies that are reviewed in this report. We note that few of these studies were available when BOTA started down this path in 2002.

Over the course of this work, we have benefited from the generous contributions of many individuals. Three members of BOTA provided the key impetus in the initial development of the ideas and the definition of the current project: Chris Edley, Daniel Koretz, and Edward Lazear. The project would never have come together without their suggestions and encouragement. In addition, the suggestions of the staff of the project's funders—Barbara Gombach and Talia Milgrom-Elcott at the Carnegie Corporation of New York, and Marshall (Mike) S. Smith at the William and Flora Hewlett Foundation—helped define a balanced and workable study. We are grateful for their suggestions for shaping the project and for their patience as the work has unfolded.

In addition to the members of BOTA, a number of individuals made invited presentations at the initial 2003 and 2005 workshops that developed the project, and we thank them: Hilda Borko, University of Colorado; Edward Deci, University of Rochester; Eric Hanushek, Stanford University; Carolyn Heinrich, University of Wisconsin, Madison; Richard Ingersoll, University of Pennsylvania; Richard Koestner, McGill University; Michael Kramer, Harvard University; Victor Lavy, Hebrew University of Jerusalem; Harry O'Neil, University of Southern California; and Brian Stecher, RAND.

The committee's workshop on multiple measures in 2007 included a number of invited presentations that helped the committee explore the use of multiple measures and refine its thinking about their use, and we are grateful for this input: Robert Bernstein, California Department of Education; Kerri Briggs, U.S. Department of Education; Mitchell Chester, Ohio Department of Education; Daniel Fuller, Association for Supervision and Curriculum Development; Drew Gitomer, Educational Testing

Service; Kati Haycock, Education Trust; Jan Hoegh, Nebraska Department of Education; Lindsay Hunsicker, Office of Senator Enzi; Robert Linn, University of Colorado; Jill Morningstar, House Education and Labor Committee; Roberto Rodriguez, Office of Senator Kennedy; and William Taylor, Citizens' Commission on Civil Rights.

As we finalized the report's text, we received assistance from a number of the authors of studies cited to ensure that we were accurately describing their study conclusions. We thank the following researchers for their assistance: Eric Bettinger, Stanford University; Thomas D. Cook, Northwestern University; Roland Fryer, Harvard University; Steven M. Glazerman, Mathematica Policy Research; Brian A. Jacob, University of Michigan; Victor Lavy, Hebrew University of Jerusalem; Jaekyung Lee, State University of New York, Buffalo; Karthik Muralidharan, University of California, San Diego; Sean F. Reardon, Stanford University; John Robert Warren, University of Minnesota; and Manyee Wong, Northwestern University.

The committee's work was assisted by members of the National Research Council (NRC) staff. Naomi Chudowsky worked closely with the committee members to turn their discussions into initial draft text. Teresia Wilmore, Kelly Duncan, Rose Neugroschel, and Kelly Iverson provided administrative support and research assistance throughout the course of the project. The text was greatly improved by the expert editing of Chris McShane, Eugenia Grohman, and Yvonne Wise. Finally, a project of this duration experiences more than its share of institutional hurdles; we are deeply indebted to the efforts of several NRC staff: Michael Feuer, Patricia Morison, Connie Citro, and Robert Hauser for their help and encouragement throughout the project.

This report has been reviewed in draft form by individuals chosen for their diverse perspectives and technical expertise, in accordance with procedures approved by the NRC Report Review Committee. The purpose of this independent review is to provide candid and critical comments that will assist the institution in making its published report as sound as possible and to ensure that the report meets institutional standards for objectivity, evidence, and responsiveness to the charge. The review comments and draft manuscript remain confidential to protect the integrity of the deliberative process.

We thank the following individuals for their review of this report: Eric Bettinger, School of Education, Stanford University; Martha Darling, consultant, Ann Arbor, MI; David P. Driscoll, consultant, Melrose, MA; Amanda M. Durik, Department of Psychology, Northern Illinois University; Edward Haertel, School of Education, Stanford University; Jane Hannaway, Education Policy Center, Urban Institute, Washington, DC; Joseph A. Martineau, Office of Educational Assessment and Accountability, Michigan Department of Education; Lorraine McDonnell, Department of Political Science, University of California at Santa Barbara; Michael S. McPherson, Office of the President, Spencer Foundation, Chicago, IL; Barbara Reskin, Department of Sociology, University of Washington; and Lauress (Laurie) L. Wise, Human Resources Research Organization (HumRRO), Monterey, CA.

Although the reviewers listed above provided many constructive comments and suggestions, they were not asked to endorse the conclusions and recommendations nor did they see the final draft of the report before its release. The review of this report was overseen by Charles E. Phelps, university professor and provost emeritus, University of Rochester and Richard J. Shavelson, School of Education, Stanford University. Appointed by the NRC, they were responsible for making certain that an independent examination of this report was carried out in accordance with institutional procedures and that all review comments were carefully considered. Responsibility for the final content of this report, however, rests entirely with the authoring committee and the institution.

Michael Hout, *Chair*
Stuart W. Elliott, *Study Director*
Committee on Incentives and Test-Based
Accountability in Public Education

Contents

Summary

In recent years, there have been increasing efforts by the federal government and the states to devise systems that make students, teachers, principals, or whole school systems accountable for how much students learn. Large-scale tests are usually a key component of such systems. The No Child Left Behind (NCLB) Act of 2001 and the widespread use of high school exit exams in many states are two examples of a trend that has been going on for several decades.

The Committee on Incentives and Test-Based Accountability in Public Education was established by the National Research Council to review and synthesize research about how incentives affect behavior and to consider the implications of that research for educational accountability systems that attach incentives to test results. The committee focused on research about incentives in which an explicit consequence is attached to a measure of performance, starting first with basic research from the social and behavioral sciences and then turning to applied research in education.

BASIC RESEARCH ABOUT INCENTIVES

In reviewing basic research from the behavioral and social sciences about how incentives operate, the committee focused on theoretical research from economics and experimental research from psychology. Together, these two literatures show the way that subtle differences in the structure of incentives can be crucial in determining their effect. The research review points to five key choices that should be considered in designing incentive systems:

1. *Who is targeted by the incentives*: In complex organizations, incentives can be designed for people in different positions who can affect outcomes in different ways.
2. *What performance measures are used*: The performance measures to which incentives are attached must be aligned with the desired outcomes for the incentives to have their desired effect.
3. *What consequences are used*: The size and structure of the consequences provided by the incentives will affect how the incentives operate and should be designed to be appropriate to the situation.
4. *What support is provided*: Without resources in support of organizational objectives, incentives can be discouraging to the very people they are intended to help, particularly if those people lack the capacity to reach the target that provides a reward or avoids a sanction.
5. *How incentives are framed and communicated*: To be effective incentives need to be framed and communicated in ways that reinforce people's commitment to the goal that incentives have been put in place to achieve, rather than in ways that erode that commitment.

The committee's research review also identified three issues related to evaluating the success of incentive systems:

1. *Nonincentivized performance measures for evaluation*: Incentives will often lead people to find ways to increase measured performance that do not also improve the desired outcomes. As a result, different performance measures—that are *not* being used in the incentives system—should be used when evaluating how the incentives are working.
2. *Changes in dispositions*: In addition to evaluating the changes in a set of defined objective outcomes, it is important to consider the way incentive systems affect people's dispositions to act when they are not being directly affected by the incentives.
3. *Weighing costs and benefits*: Incentive systems will typically generate a mix of costs and benefits that have to be weighed against each other to determine the net value of the system.

TESTS AS PERFORMANCE MEASURES

The tests that are typically used to measure performance in education fall short of providing a complete measure of desired educational outcomes in many ways. This is important because the use of incentives for performance on tests is likely to reduce emphasis on the outcomes that are not measured by the test.

The academic tests used with test-based incentives obviously do not directly measure performance in untested subjects and grade levels or development of such characteristics as curiosity and persistence. However, those tests also fall short in measuring performance in the *tested* subjects and grades in important ways. Some aspects of performance in many tested subjects are difficult or even impossible to assess with current tests. And even for aspects of performance that can be tested, practical constraints on the length and cost of testing make it necessary to limit the content and types of questions. As a result, tests can measure only a subset of the content of a tested subject.

When incentives encourage teachers to focus narrowly on the material included on a particular test, scores on the tested portion of the content standards may increase while understanding of the untested portion of the content standards may stay the same or decrease. To the extent feasible, it is important to broaden the range of material included on tests to better reflect the full range of what students are expected to know and be able to do. And it is important to remember that the scores on the tests used with incentives may give an inflated picture of learning with respect to the full range of the content standards.

Incentives for educators are rarely attached directly to individual test scores; rather, they are usually attached to an indicator that combines and summarizes those scores in some way. Attaching consequences to different indicators created from the same test scores can produce dramatically different incentives. For example, an indicator constructed from average test scores or average test score gains will be sensitive to changes at all levels of achievement. In contrast, an indicator constructed from the percentage of students who meet a performance standard will be affected only by changes in the achievement of the students near the cut score defining the performance standard.

Given the broad outcomes that are the goals for education, the necessarily limited coverage of tests, and the ways that indicators constructed from tests focus on particular types of information, it is prudent to consider designing an incentive system that uses multiple performance measures. Incentive systems in other sectors have evolved toward using increasing numbers of performance measures on the basis of their experience with the limitations of particular performance measures. Over time, organizations look for a set of performance measures that better covers the full range of desired outcomes and also monitors behavior that would merely inflate the measures without improving outcomes.

INCENTIVE PROGRAMS REVIEWED

The committee's literature review focused on studies that allowed us to draw causal conclusions about the overall effects of test-based incentive programs. We looked specifically for information about outcomes *other* than the high-stakes tests that have incentives attached in order to avoid having our conclusions biased by the test score inflation that the incentives may have caused. We also attempted to contrast different incentive programs according to the key features identified by the basic research in economic theory (the first four features noted above): who is targeted by the incentives, what performance measures are used, what consequences are used, and what support is provided. The existing literature did not allow us to contrast incentive programs according to the way they frame and communicate incentives, the key feature identified by the basic research in psychology (the fifth feature noted above).

We focused on 15 test-based incentive programs, including the large-scale policies of NCLB, its predecessors, and state high school exit exams, as well as a number of experiments and programs carried out in both the United States and other countries. These various programs involved a number of different incentive designs and substantial numbers of schools, teachers, and students.

CONCLUSIONS

Conclusion 1: Test-based incentive programs, as designed and implemented in the programs that have been carefully studied, have not increased student achievement enough to bring the United States close to the levels of the highest achieving countries. When evaluated using relevant low-stakes tests, which are less likely to be inflated by the incentives themselves, the overall effects on achievement tend to be small and are effectively zero for a number of programs. Even when evaluated using the tests attached to the incentives, a number of programs show only small effects. Programs in foreign countries that show larger effects are not clearly applicable in the U.S. context. School-level incentives like those of the No Child Left Behind Act produce some of the larger estimates of achievement effects, with effect sizes around 0.08 standard deviations, but the measured effects to date tend to be concentrated in elementary grade mathematics and the effects are small compared to the improvements the nation hopes to achieve.

Conclusion 2: The evidence we have reviewed suggests that high school exit exam programs, as currently implemented in

the United States, decrease the rate of high school graduation without increasing achievement. The best available estimate suggests a decrease of 2 percentage points when averaged over the population. In contrast, several experiments with providing incentives for graduation in the form of rewards, while keeping graduation standards constant, suggest that such incentives might be used to increase high school completion.

RECOMMENDATIONS FOR POLICY AND RESEARCH

The modest and variable benefits shown by test-based incentive programs to date suggest that such programs should be used with caution and that substantial further research is required to understand how they can be used successfully.

Recommendation 1: Despite using them for several decades, policy makers and educators do not yet know how to use test-based incentives to consistently generate positive effects on achievement and to improve education. Policy makers should support the development and evaluation of promising new models that use test-based incentives in more sophisticated ways as one aspect of a richer accountability and improvement process. However, the modest success of incentive programs to date means that all use of test-based incentives should be carefully studied to help determine which forms of incentives are successful in education and which are not. Continued experimentation with test-based incentives should not displace investment in the development of other aspects of the education system that are important complements to the incentives themselves and likely to be necessary for incentives to be effective in improving education.

Recommendation 2: Policy makers and researchers should design and evaluate new test-based incentive programs in ways that provide information about alternative approaches to incentives and accountability. This should include exploration of the effects of key features suggested by basic research, such as who is targeted for incentives; what performance measures are used; what consequences are attached to the performance measures and how frequently they are used; what additional support and options are provided to schools, teachers, and students in their efforts to improve; and how incentives are framed and communicated. Choices among the options for some or all of these features are likely to be critical in determining which—if any—incentive programs are successful.

Recommendation 3: Research about the effects of incentive programs should fully document the structure of each program and should evaluate a broad range of outcomes. To avoid having their results determined by the score inflation that occurs in the high-stakes tests attached to the incentives, researchers should use low-stakes tests that do not mimic the high-stakes tests to evaluate how test-based incentives affect achievement. Other outcomes, such as later performance in education or work and dispositions related to education, are also important to study. To help explain why test-based incentives sometimes produce negative effects on achievement, researchers should collect data on changes in educational practice by the people who are affected by the incentives.

1

Introduction

In recent years there have been increasing efforts by the federal government and the states to devise systems that make students, teachers, principals, or whole school systems accountable for how much students learn. Large-scale tests are usually a key component of such systems. The No Child Left Behind (NCLB) Act of 2001, a prominent example of such efforts, is the continuation of a steady trend toward greater test-based accountability that has been going on for decades. The use of high school exit exams by many states as a requirement for receiving a diploma is another example. Still another example is the widespread interest in using student test scores as a way of rating and rewarding teachers and principals.

Test-based accountability systems provide policy makers with potentially powerful but blunt tools to influence what happens in local schools and classrooms. These policies attach consequences to assessments by holding educators and students accountable for achieving at certain levels on tests. When schools, teachers, or students score below performance cutoffs on tests, they often face sanctions, and when they perform well, they are sometimes rewarded. After reviewing policy and practice, Richard Elmore (2004) concluded that test-based accountability has been more enduring than any other policy in the field of education for at least the past 50 years and that it is unlikely to recede in the foreseeable future. Test-based accountability continues to dominate the policy agenda at the federal, state, and local levels—"a remarkable accomplishment in a political environment where reform agendas typically have shifted from year to year" according to Michael Feuer (2008, p. 274).

BACKGROUND

The test-based accountability movement in education can be seen as part of a broader movement for government reform and accountability over the past few decades that has sought to measure and publicize government performance as a way to improve it. The Government Performance and Results Act of 1993 is an example of the more general trend in the United States, and there are similar examples in many other countries.

> While the broad objectives of these reforms to promote more "effective, efficient, and responsive government" are the same as those of reforms introduced more than a century ago, what is new are the increasing scope, sophistication, and external visibility of performance measurement activities, impelled by legislative requirements aimed at holding governments accountable for *outcomes*. (Heinrich, 2003, p. 25)

In education, accountability systems in the United States have attached ever-stronger incentives to tests over time. Tests for accountability purposes emerged under Title I of the Elementary and Secondary Education Act (ESEA) of 1965 and the start of the National Assessment of Educational Progress (NAEP). However, the original form of these national requirements for testing did not include explicit incentives linked to test results (Koretz and Hamilton, 2006; Shepard, 2008). In the 1970s, the minimum competency movement led to greater consequences being attached to the results of tests for students, with graduation and promotion decisions in some states being tied to test results. The 1988 reauthorization of ESEA required Title I schools with stagnant or declining test scores to file improvement plans with their districts.

The standards-based reform movement of the early 1990s led to the requirement in the 1994 ESEA reauthorization for states to create rigorous content and performance standards and report student test results in terms of the standards (National Research Council, 1997, p. 25). This was followed by the requirements of the 2001 reauthorization (NCLB) for schools and districts to show progress in the proportion of students reaching proficiency or to face the possibility of restructuring. The emergence of value-added modeling led to increasing interest in the use of test results for evaluating and rewarding individual teachers and principals (National Research Council and National Academy of Education, 2010).

This brief sketch of test-based accountability in education over a 50-year period condenses a complicated and fitful history into a few pivotal points. In some cases changes at the national level were preceded by changes in individual states, and over the decades there were periodic waves of concern about education that included the reaction to Sputnik in 1957, the publication of *A Nation at Risk* (National Commission on Excellence in Education, 1983), and responses to the U.S. position on the international comparative tests that became available in the late 1990s and 2000s.

This report does not attempt to provide a detailed history of the growing use of explicit incentives that are attached to tests. Rather, it reviews what social and behavioral scientists have learned about motivation and incentives over the same period that test-based incentives have spread. In response to the charge to the committee, the goal of the report is to inform education policy makers about the use of such incentives and to recommend ways that their use in test-based accountability systems can be improved.

COMMITTEE CHARGE AND REPORT SCOPE

The Committee on Incentives and Test-Based Accountability in Public Education was established by the National Research Council (NRC) with support from the Carnegie Corporation of New York and the William and Flora Hewlett Foundation. The committee's charge was to review and synthesize research about how incentives affect behavior that would have implications for educational accountability systems that attach incentives to test results.

The project originated in the recognition that there is important research about what happens when incentives are attached to measures of performance. Much of this research has been conducted outside the field of education and so is unlikely to be familiar to education policy makers. As they increasingly turn to the use of incentives in test-based accountability systems, their efforts should be informed by the findings from that research.

The goals of the committee's study are to (1) help identify circumstances in which test-based incentives may have a positive or a negative impact on student learning, (2) recommend ways to improve the use of test-based incentives in current accountability policies, and (3) highlight the most important directions for further research about the use of test-based incentives in education.

In order to make the study feasible, it was necessary for the committee to focus its approach to addressing the charge with respect to how we would consider incentives, accountability, and recent research about the use of test-based incentives in education.

Incentives The committee focused on research related to incentives in which an explicit consequence is attached to a measure of performance. Although it can be difficult in some cases to draw a precise line between consequences that are explicit and those that are not, this rough contrast provided a practical way to focus the study in the current policy environment where there is substantial interest in test-based incentives that clearly have explicit consequences. We did not use a broader interpretation of the term "incentive," which could have encompassed all determinants of behavior and required a literature review that included all fields in the social and behavioral sciences.

Accountability The committee focused on research related to the use of test-based incentives for education accountability. We excluded both other types of accountability in education and a conceptual approach for contrasting those other approaches with test-based accountability.

Recent Research on Test-Based Incentives in Education The committee focused on two kinds of research: (1) basic research that has been conducted in the social and behavioral sciences with potential application to many different settings, including education, and (2) research on test-based incentives in education. For both kinds of work, we focused primarily on research that allows us to draw causal inferences about the overall effect of test-based incentives.

The committee's entire effort could have been consumed by a broader approach to any one of these three elements. Only by judiciously limiting the focus on each one could we appropriately address our overall charge, which is to make policy makers aware of key findings about the use of incentives and the potential implications of these findings for the design of test-based accountability systems in education.

We note that our focus on incentives that involve the attachment of explicit consequences to test results specifically excludes the broader role that test results can play in informing educators and the public about the performance of the educational system and thereby providing stimulus for improvement. We understand that some readers would have wanted us to have broadened our treatment of "explicit consequences" to have included the publication of test results with its potential of both motivating educators to improve and driving policy pressure for reform. In the end, we did not have the capacity to adequately broaden the study in this way, which would have required a much richer treatment of incentive effects, types of accountability, and methods of research about education. We are sympathetic with the arguments that the information from test results is likely to affect both teachers and policy makers. However, we note that there have been many arguments and proposed policies over the past decade or two that have taken as their starting point a conclusion that mere information has been insufficient to drive educational improvement (e.g., National Research Council, 1996). The result has been a strong focus in education policy on the importance of attaching explicit consequences to test results. That is the type of test-based incentives that our study examines.

In addition, we note that our literature review is necessarily limited by the types of incentive programs that have been implemented and studied. Given the intense interest in the use of incentives over the past decade, there are incentive programs that are too new to have been evaluated by researchers, and there are interesting proposals for incentive programs that have not yet been implemented. We mention some of these new programs and proposals throughout the report, but we obviously cannot draw any conclusions about their effectiveness at this time.

It has been more than a decade since the landmark National Research Council (1999) report, *High Stakes: Testing for Tracking, Promotion, and Graduation*, was issued. That report contains a number of cautions about the use of student tests for making high-stakes decisions for students, with notable recommendations about the importance of using multiple sources of information for any important decision about students and the necessity of providing adequate instructional support before high-stakes tests are given. *High Stakes* cited a "strong need for better evidence on the intended benefits and unintended negative consequences of using high-stakes tests to make decisions about individuals," particularly with respect to evidence about "whether the consequences of a particular test use are educationally beneficial for students—for example, by increasing academic achievement or reducing dropout rates" (p. 8). In the years since *High Stakes* was published, the use of test-based incentives has continued to grow, and researchers have made important advances in their evaluations of those evaluations. This report looks at what we have learned as a result.

Chapter 2 reviews findings from two complementary areas of research in the behavioral and social sciences about the operation of incentives: theoretical work from economics about using performance-based incentives and experimental results from psychology on motivation and external rewards. Chapter 3 looks at the use of tests as performance measures that have incentives attached to them, considering some key ways the effect of incentives is influenced by the characteristics of the tests and the performance measures that are constructed from test results. Chapter 4 reviews research about the use of test-based incentives within education, specifically looking at accountability policies with consequences for schools, teachers, and students. Chapter 5 concludes with the committee's recommendations for policy and research.

STUDY CONTEXT

It is important to note two aspects of the context for our work, although they may seem obvious. First, throughout the report, we focus on one part—the incentives—of a test-based accountability system, which is itself only one part of the larger education system. Our focus was driven by our charge, not because incentives are the only important part of a test-based accountability system or the only important part of the education system. Researchers have proposed a number of elements that are likely to be needed for a test-based accountability system to work effectively in the overall education system (see, e.g., Baker and Linn, 2003; Feuer, 2008; Fuhrman, 2004; Haertel and Herman, 2005; O'Day, 2004). In addition to the role played by incentives themselves, researchers have noted the importance of clear goals, appropriate educational standards, tests aligned to the standards and suitable for accountability purposes, helpful test reporting, available alternative actions and teaching methods to improve student learning, and the capacity of educators to apply those alternative actions and teaching methods. Although we note at some points the importance of these elements in allowing test-based incentives to change behavior in ways that will improve student learning, at many points in the report the importance of these other elements is left unstated and should be inferred by the reader.

Second, this study was conducted at a time of widespread interest in NCLB, which is currently the most visible education accountability system in the United States. As a result, NCLB forms a backdrop for much of the policy interest in the effects of incentives, and readers may at some point view this report as a critique of that law. However, the study was not intended or conducted as a critique or evaluation of NCLB. As noted above, NCLB is a continuation of a broader trend toward the use of stronger test-based incentives that has been going on for decades. This study is focused on evidence related to that broader trend, not on particular aspects of a specific law. In particular, we view our report as a resource for policy makers looking to the future of accountability, not as an evaluation of any particular past practice or program.

2

Basic Research on Incentives

A broad interpretation of "incentive" could encompass all determinants of behavior and require a literature review that includes all fields in the social and behavioral sciences. As explained in Chapter 1, the committee focused on research related to incentives in which an explicit consequence—either positive or negative—is attached to a measure of performance and on two areas that together provide a complementary picture of what we know about their effects: theoretical research from economics about using performance-based incentives and experimental research from psychology on motivation and external rewards.[1]

The work from economics provides a framework for understanding how the effect of incentives can vary from context to context and from person to person. The work from psychology provides empirical results showing how the behavior caused by incentives can vary from context to context and from person to person. Together, these two literatures provide a picture of the complexity of the structure of incentives and an understanding of the subtle differences in their design that can be crucial in determining their effects. Although we use these two research literatures to structure our analysis, we also discuss some empirical results from economics, sociology, and personnel psychology where they are applicable.

---

[1]Although the committee focused in particular on theoretical work from economics and empirical work from psychology, we recognize that this division is artificial since the research in both fields includes complementary theoretical and empirical work. Where appropriate, the chapter notes related empirical work in economics and theoretical work in psychology.

ECONOMIC THEORY AND ISSUES

Economics has a well-developed body of theoretical research that looks at how organizational incentives should be designed and uses the results of that work to understand why different organizations use different incentives. This body of research applies the general economic approach of explaining human behavior as resulting from individuals' trying to get the best outcomes for themselves within the constraints of their environments. This general framework for understanding human behavior has proven to be quite powerful, although there are critiques that it misses important aspects of human psychology that limit the ability to determine the best outcome in the idealized way that economists assume (see, e.g., Ariely, 2008; Rabin, 1998).

The research on the use of incentives in organizations extends the general economic framework by analyzing differences in the objectives of the individuals who make up an organization. In particular, the work contrasts the objective of an organization as a whole—as defined by the owner or "principal" of that organization—with the objective of an individual worker or "agent." As a very basic example, an owner probably cares about the organization's overall profit while the workers care about their own pay, hours of work, and levels of effort. Because of the difference in these objectives, a worker in an organization may not behave in ways that will best achieve the owner's goals for the organization—which can make the organization less productive and thereby make things worse for the workers indirectly by reducing employment or pay in the long run. To help correct such a situation, incentives can be used to encourage the workers to work toward the owner's goals for the organization.

The classic example of the effect of incentive structures is to contrast the effect of paying workers by the hour with the effect of paying them by the amount of work they perform measured by some quantity of output. The latter is often known as a "piece rate," derived from a manufacturing context in which a worker is paid for each piece produced. The owner of the company will want the workers to produce more per hour in order to increase profits: switching to a piece rate gives the worker an incentive to do so; paying by the hour may not do so. Sales commissions are one of the well-known ways in which piece rates are currently used in many industries. Empirical research has shown many situations in which simple piece rate incentives operate as the economic theory predicts (Prendergast, 1999), although the efficiency of incentives depends on the precise social relations that tend to grow up around piece work (see Burawoy, 1979; Sallaz, 2009).

Beyond the basic difference between paying by the hour and by the piece, there are important and subtle complexities that affect the way incentives operate. A number of contrasts in incentive structures provide some understanding about the ways that incentives work in different settings or for different people. In the rest of this section, we discuss five different types of complexity that have been analyzed and the important considerations they raise for the design of incentives in education:

1. finding performance measures,
2. the different effects of incentives on different people,
3. the effects of uncertainty and control,
4. the effects of working in groups, and
5. weighing the benefits of incentives against their costs.

Finding Performance Measures to Use with Incentives

In most jobs, the value of the work performed by each worker is difficult to assess. For example, for many jobs, it is hard to measure what workers produce because their output cannot be counted in any meaningful way. The qualitative aspects of that work—the relationship with the client, the clarity of the report, the accuracy of the numbers—are more important in determining its value than such countable outcomes as the number of meetings held, pages written, or spreadsheets produced.

The difficulty in measuring the true results of what workers do is an important constraint in providing incentives—and the difference between the available measures of workers' output and the true value of that output has consequences for the way incentives operate. In an attempt to provide appropriate incentives, organizations often look for performance measures to use in objectively quantifying what each worker is producing. The problem is that these performance measures necessarily focus on the aspects of the job that can be easily quantified and neglect the qualitative aspects of the job that cannot be easily quantified. When incentives are attached to these performance measures, the predictable result is that workers often focus on the readily quantifiable aspects of the job that affect the performance measures and neglect the quantitative and qualitative aspects of the job that do not factor into the performance measures.

There are numerous examples of the distortion that results from the use of incentives with performance measures that do not adequately reflect the true value of the work that is being done. These examples confirm the findings in the theoretical analyses about the problems that can result when incentives are attached to performance measures that are not closely aligned with the true value of the work. For example, computer programmers rewarded by the length of their programs write longer programs, surgeons penalized for high mortality rates take less risky cases, and chief executive officers (CEOs) rewarded for their company's earning performance manipulate those earnings reports (Prendergast, 1999; Rothstein, 2008).

A good example of this kind of result in education occurs when incentives are attached to the number of "proficient" students: the result is that extra attention is given to the students who are just below the threshold of proficiency, while teachers and schools may compete for the proficient students who do not bring the threat of negative consequences. Another example can be seen when college rankings reward a more selective admissions policy: the result is that college recruiters encourage applicants from unqualified students because they will effectively get credit for rejecting them (Stevens, 2007).

In these examples, the incentives placed on the performance measures lead workers to perform actions that increase the performance measures but not the underlying value of their work. It is typical for performance measures to become distorted when they are used for incentive purposes. This is a version of the phenomenon sometimes referred to as Campbell's law (Campbell, 1975, p. 49):

> The more any quantitative social indicator is used for social decision making, the more subject it will be to corruption pressures and the more apt it will be to distort and corrupt the social processes it is intended to monitor.

In organizations seeking to find an appropriate incentives scheme, the performance measures used may evolve over time in the search for measures that are well aligned with the true value that the workers produce. For example, the Job Training Partnership Act of 1982 initially provided incentives for local employment and training centers that were based on job placement rates and the wages at the time of placement. These incentives led the centers to focus on people with stronger work histories who were more likely to find work and to be paid more. The program then added performance measures focused on people with weaker work histories and on changes in earnings. The successor to this act, the Workforce Investment Act, currently uses a combination of 17 performance measures to provide incentives to local employment and training centers (Heinrich and Marschke, 2010). Similar evolution in performance measures has occurred in other areas in which performance incentives have been used, such as in health care (see Rothstein, 2008).

In education, many incentives are currently focused on a narrow set of measures derived from annual test results in grades 3-8 in reading and mathematics. This focus falls far short of a complete measure of desired educational outcomes. Most notably, it omits entirely such things as advanced levels of performance in the two tested subjects; areas of performance in those subjects that are hard to assess with standardized tests;

performance in other subjects and other grades; growth in such important characteristics as creativity, curiosity, persistence, values, collaboration, and socialization; and the eventual success of students in graduating, obtaining postsecondary education, finding productive and satisfying work, and contributing as members of their communities.

The challenge of finding appropriate performance measures to use with incentives is often made more difficult by the challenge of defining the underlying goals that one wants the performance measures to reflect. For many organizations, it can be difficult or impossible to specify the organization's goals in a way that would satisfy all stakeholders. This can be true not only for such institutions as not-for-profit organizations, government agencies, and schools, but also for groups and individuals in for-profit firms. For example, different stakeholders in a for-profit energy corporation may disagree about whether to focus on fossil fuels or on the development of renewable energy sources.

In education, schools are responsible for educating students in many ways: fostering cognitive skills, emotional and physical development, readiness for work and civic participation, as well as students' health and safety. In addition, schools are charged with ensuring that all students meet some minimal standards and that some of them are able to meet very high standards. Although these goals are not inconsistent, they all compete for the limited education resources that are available and, ultimately, require schools to make difficult tradeoffs among them (Dixit, 2002). These trade-offs affect the design of the accountability system. Ideally, one would like to have at least one performance measure linked to each goal, but this ideal is often not practical to carry out. Consequently, further trade-offs in the selection of performance measures are generally called for. Finally, within the set of performance measures that will be used, it is necessary to decide how heavily to weight each measure in the overall incentives system. This added challenge of reaching a consensus about an organization's objective that can be captured in a set of feasible performance measures compounds the difficulty of finding appropriate measures that are aligned with that objective.

A theoretical analysis shows that an optimal incentives scheme will place less weight on performance measures that are less aligned with the true value of what the workers produce (Baker, 2002). What is critical is not whether there is an overall correlation between the performance measures and the workers' true productivity, but whether they are correlated "at the margin"—that is, correlated for additional changes from the status quo—so that the actions that improve the measures also improve the workers' underlying productivity.

The distinction between an overall correlation and a correlation at the margin is especially important because of the distortion in performance measures that occurs when incentives are attached to them. A performance measure may be generally correlated with the full range of outcomes without incentives—so that high levels of the measure are associated with overall good performance—but when incentives are attached to the performance measure, the actions taken to increase the performance measure on the margin may not increase overall performance at all. This common outcome is referred to as "gaming" the system or the test. Test preparation classes are an example of this phenomenon: knowing when to guess at the answer and when to skip the question will improve a score without increasing learning in the domain of the test (Koretz, 2008b).

In education, it is not clear how strong the current incentives are. Objectively they may seem small, because they rarely involve serious consequences, like substantial bonuses or decertification in the case of teachers. However, studies of cheating by teachers suggest that some of them react very strongly to the seemingly small incentives in the current system (see Chapter 4). It is also important to keep in mind, as noted below, that any given set of incentives will have different effects in different settings and for different people, causing some people to work harder or more effectively and others to give up or to work in ways that thwart an organization's goals.

Distortion is virtually unavoidable in an incentives system that uses performance measures that do not reflect the full value of workers' productivity. And as noted above, few jobs lend themselves to comprehensive measurement, so one should usually expect some distortion and take steps to minimize it. In education, one example of distortion occurs when teachers and students focus narrowly on tested material and ignore topics that are not covered on the tests.

In evaluating an incentives system, it is important to evaluate, not whether distortion exists, but whether the incentives result in a sufficient increase in the output desired to justify the costs of running the incentives system, including the costs of monitoring the performance measures, providing the incentives, and addressing the unintended, negative effects. Because of the distortion in performance measures that results from placing incentives on those measures, the true change in the output that results from the incentives system cannot be determined by looking at changes in the performance measures being used in the system, but must be determined by looking at *other* indicators of performance. In an educational setting using test-based incentives, this means that it is necessary to look at other tests besides the tests attached to the consequences—other tests that are not themselves designed to mimic the high-stakes test—in order to determine how the incentives are affecting achievement.

As a result of the difficulty in measuring results, most organizations base their incentives on subjective rather than objective measures or on some combination of the two (Prendergast, 1999; Rothstein, 2008). Subjective measures have the potential to provide a more complete assessment of the contribution of each worker, with the ability to appropriately take into account special circumstances and to discount the value of quantitative measures that may be influenced by gaming behavior. Of course, there are problems with subjective measures, including that their reliability and validity are affected by such things as the reluctance of supervisors to differentiate workers in their performance assessments, the information that is privately held by workers about their own effort and performance, and the attempts of workers to game the measures by spending time to influence their supervisors' assessments. These difficulties will be compounded in settings, such as schools, that do not face strong pressure to produce good results and may have personnel policies that discourage differentiation of workers on the basis of their performance. Systems that rely on subjective performance measures must have or must create incentives for the relevant authorities (e.g., principals) to act on their subjective assessments, while protecting the workers from arbitrary—or even capricious—evaluations.

The Different Effects of Incentives on Different People

One of the important results in the economic theory about incentives is that the effect of a particular incentives structure is likely to be different for different people. Although incentives are often structured so that everyone is given the same target, the target will often be easy for some people to meet but hard for others (Lazear, 2000). As a result, the effect of the incentive is likely to differ, encouraging greater performance for those people who are able to reach the target with some extra effort but discouraging performance for those people who believe they are unlikely to reach the target at all.[2]

This differential effect can lead in turn to differential turnover across a group of people receiving incentives: over time, an organization that uses performance incentives is likely to attract and retain workers who can achieve the targets that are rewarded by the incentives, while workers who are unlikely to be successful will become discouraged and leave. Research shows this differential effect of incentives on people. For example, Lazear (2000) studied a change from hourly to piece-rate pay for workers who install windshields in cars: he found that productivity improved by 35 percent, one-third of which was produced by lower productivity workers leaving the firm and being replaced by higher productivity workers.

---

[2]See the discussion in the section "Psychological Results and Issues" below about the effects of low and high targets.

The knowledge that incentives will have different effects on different people depending on their ability to achieve the targets can be readily applied to examples within education. Lazear (2006) applies the theory to the case of incentives given to teachers—in a model in which teachers differ in their effectiveness in raising student test scores—and produces the result that incentives will cause some teachers to increase their effort and others to change occupations. In Lazear's model, this differential reaction would lead to increasing effectiveness in the pool of teachers over time— as measured by the ability of the teachers to raise test scores—because the ones who leave are those who are less able to respond effectively to the incentives.[3] Similarly, economic theory suggests that incentives given to students—such as high school exit exams—will cause the students who have greater ability to pass the test, but can only pass it with increased effort, to increase their effort while causing the students who have less ability to pass the test to drop out (Betts and Costrell, 2001). If exit exams are introduced without making other adjustments to provide remediation and support to students who will have difficulty passing the test, the differential reaction could lead to increasing achievement in students who graduate and increasing numbers of students who do not graduate. (Chapter 4 looks at the literature related to these responses by students and teachers in more detail.)

In the teacher and student examples just mentioned, the economic models assume that the actions available to the teachers and students are either to increase effort or quit. A similar model of the different reactions to test-based incentives might consider instead that the two actions available are different versions of "increasing effort"—one involving greater focus on the full curriculum and the other involving extra time in test preparation. A model of teacher and student reactions to test-based incentives—in which different teachers and students have different abilities to be successful on the tests by focusing on the full curriculum or different beliefs about what instructional strategy would be successful— would show that the same incentives structure could lead to an increased attention to the full curriculum for some teachers and students while also leading to increased attention to test preparation by others. Teachers and students who believed they could be successful on tests by focusing on the full curriculum might choose to do so in such a model, while others might choose instead to focus on test preparation.

---

[3]Research related to teacher turnover has shown that the teachers who leave teaching before their second year tend to be worse than the average teacher, as measured by changes in student test scores (Boyd et al., 2009). This research was conducted under the general approach to school-based accountability under the No Child Left Behind Act; we are not aware of any research comparing types of teacher turnover occurring with stronger and weaker teacher incentives.

As noted in the previous section (and discussed in more detail in Chapter 3), a focus on test preparation is likely to distort the test scores, resulting in an increase in the scores that is inflated as a measure of the true learning in the domain. So in this alternative model the same incentive might lead to test score increases for both groups of teachers and students, but the actions producing those score increases and the true learning involved would be dramatically different for the two groups. Importantly, these differences would be invisible without gathering additional information beyond the test score data.

Effects of Uncertainty and Control in Providing Incentives

In most jobs, both the value of what workers produce and the measures of that value can be strongly affected by many factors that the workers themselves do not control. For example, a client might be very motivated or not, or budget constraints may limit options for improvements that are needed. As a result, if an employer uses incentives, it is likely that the payoffs will vary according to those other factors, in addition to varying because of the workers' own efforts. However, people generally dislike uncertainty, and if their pay is going to be influenced by factors they cannot control, they will want a higher level of pay on average to compensate for that uncertainty.

A theoretical analysis shows that an optimal incentives scheme will place less weight on performance measures that are subject to greater uncertainty because they are subject to factors that the workers do not control (Baker, 2002). The use of such performance measures will require firms to pay their workers a higher average level of pay because the workers will need to be compensated for the greater uncertainty in their pay in comparison with what they would receive at another job. Although the firm may benefit on average from the response of the workers to the incentives, the higher level of average pay that workers need to compensate them for the uncertainty will reduce the extent to which the firm uses incentives. If the workers are adverse to the uncertainty associated with such performance measures, it may not be worthwhile for the firm to use incentives because the benefit from the increased productivity of the workers due to the incentives may be less than the cost of the higher average pay needed to compensate them for the uncertainty.

In education, many factors affect student learning that teachers and schools do not directly control, including, in particular, many aspects of students' home environments. As a result, the learning that occurs in the classroom of an individual teacher can vary widely from student to student and from year to year. As a result of this uncertainty and variability in student outcomes, many teachers dislike incentives based on student outcomes and will need to be compensated at a higher average level to make up for this uncertainty. Although there are things schools can do to affect or work around aspects of students' home environments—such as working with parents or providing breakfast or study time at school—such interventions are not likely to be sufficient to counteract the variability in home environments across students. There is also strong evidence of random year-to-year fluctuations in student performance even at the school level, perhaps because one year the test happens to ask more questions that were covered in the school's curriculum or because of common environmental factors, such as whether there was an important school basketball game the night before the exam (Kane and Staiger, 2002).

In many jobs, workers are compared with each other as a way of reducing the effect of factors that the workers themselves do not control. The argument is that workers in similar jobs will be subject to similar uncertainties that are beyond their control. So, for example, CEOs may be judged by the performance of their company's stock price compared with other companies in the same industry as a way of controlling for changes in the industry that are outside the control of each CEO. The technique of comparing workers with each other rather than to an objective standard is often used in promotions, which is one of the most common ways of providing incentives in firms (Prendergast, 1999). In education, the approach of comparing teachers or schools with each other could address common year-to-year changes, like fluctuations in test difficulty, but it would not account for the most important year-to-year changes, which occur at the student level and so do not affect every teacher in the same way. Many researchers are currently working on "value-added" techniques, which statistically adjust for differences at the student level to make it possible to compare the results of different teachers. However, as noted in Chapter 3, it is not yet clear how fully these models can account for student differences to provide accurate measures of teacher effectiveness.

Effects of Groups in Providing Incentives

Economic theory has also looked at some of the issues in designing incentives for groups of people rather than for individuals. In many jobs, workers need to work together in a team (or group), and the results of their work depend on the contributions of all the members. There are inevitable tradeoffs in the available measures of the workers' contributions. On the one hand, any measures of the work done by individual workers will miss their contributions to the work of the other team members and so will give an inaccurate assessment of that worker's total productivity. On the other hand, performance measures based on the productivity for the entire team will be very uncertain indicators of the performance of any single worker because they will depend on the performance of all members of the team. In this situation, there is a tension between using inaccurate individual performance measures that ignore each worker's contributions to the team and using team performance measures that vary because of the performance of all the team members and therefore provide only weak incentives to each worker. Whether it is better to provide incentives at the individual or team level in this situation depends on the relative importance of cooperation by the team members and the degree of uncertainty added by using a team performance measure (Baker, 2002).

In education, student learning is affected by many other people besides the designated teacher for a class, including other teachers, students' parents, and students' peers. In addition, there are important opportunities for teachers to contribute to the teaching skills of their colleagues, thereby affecting the learning of their colleagues' students indirectly. (Chapter 4 discusses results of studies providing incentives to teachers, including experiments that compared the effects of incentives provided to individual teachers and to all teachers as a group in a school.)

Research outside economics raises issues about the functioning of organizations that go beyond the issues addressed by economic theory. For example, sociological research deals with the structure of organizations and the formation of occupational norms. Even in schools in which teachers do not appear to be working together or working with each other's students, there are still important group processes that influence how any external incentives are interpreted and communicated among all the teachers. Organizational theory describes schools as "loosely coupled" organizations that buffer classroom practice from change and outside scrutiny and therefore respond to outside pressures by making largely symbolic changes (Firestone, 1985; Meyer and Rowan, 1977, 1978; Weick, 1976).

The standards-based accountability movement recognized these tendencies and sought to counter them. A call for systemic reform by Smith and O'Day (1990) argued that a "fundamental barrier to developing and sustaining successful schools in the USA is the fragmented, complex multi-layered educational policy system in which they are embedded" (p. 237). The systemic reform strategy aimed to overcome loosely coupled organizational structures through state-led education reform that emphasized unified goals, a coherent system of instructional guidance, and restructured educational governance. Some of the concrete manifestations of this approach have included school-level efforts to coordinate, support, and monitor instruction by changes to emphasize principals' roles as instructional leaders, promote mentoring relationships among teachers, and institute coaching models for teacher improvement.

Organizational theories predicted that the shift toward systemic reform would lead to greater tightening among goals, activities, and outcomes, but they also predicted that enormous inertia would have to be overcome for this shift to occur (Rowan and Miskel, 1999). Teaching in low-performing schools is difficult; maintaining a proper learning environment can reduce the teaching opportunities. These are the environments the reforms seek to change, yet, on a daily basis, it remains unclear how to assert the precedence of teaching over establishing order.

The economic theory that analyzes the contrast between individual and group incentives only crudely approximates the functioning of incentives as described in the sociological research about schools as organizations. The sociological work considers many incentives that do not involve explicitly defined consequences, and it raises the problem of understanding how the effects of incentives may or may not be communicated informally from one member of an organization to another. The combined message coming from economics and sociology about the operation of incentives in groups is that it is necessary to think beyond the effect of direct incentives on individuals in an organization: in addition, one has to consider the extent to which the work is done jointly and the extent to which the effect of any direct incentives will be informally transmitted to other members of the group.

In an organizational structure as complicated as a school system, there are many people playing different roles and interacting with each other in complicated ways. In such a system, explicit incentives might be introduced at a number of different points. In Chapter 4, we consider test-based incentives that are placed on schools, teachers, or students, although the incentives offered to any one of these parts of the system are likely to be transmitted informally to the others to some extent. If explicit incentives are targeted to individuals rather than groups, then there may be some value in offering incentives to people who are relatively higher in the hierarchy and potentially have the ability to transmit the incentives in ways that encourage cooperative behavior. For example, explicit incentives for principals could lead to informal group incentives for teachers. At the same time, there are different actions available to the people who play different roles: principals can have a direct effect on hiring decisions, but they can affect instruction only indirectly by working through teachers; teachers have a direct effect on instruction, but they can affect student effort and attention only indirectly by working through students. To the extent that the informal transmission of incentives in an organization is imperfect, it is important to consider what behavior one is trying to change and who has the ability to affect that behavior directly.

Weighing the Costs and Benefits of Incentives

The considerations above all raise the likelihood that there will be tradeoffs that need to be considered in deciding whether to use explicit incentives and, if so, figuring out how they should be structured. It is hardly surprising to assert that there will be both benefits and costs—positive and negative effects—from the use of incentives and that these should be weighed against each other. However, it can often be difficult to acknowledge the need for tradeoffs in policy discussions. And, once acknowledged, it can also often be quite difficult to figure out how to weigh the benefits and costs.

Considering the challenge of finding appropriate performance measures to use with incentives, it is important to recognize that the presence of distortion from the use of imperfect performance measures does not automatically imply that a performance-based incentives system should not be used. The use of imperfect performance measures means that there will be some distortion in behavior, which will make it more difficult to determine the benefits of the system (because other performance measures must be used) and which will cause some parts of the system to work less productively than they would have in the absence of the incentives. However, it may still be the case that the incentives system produces a substantial benefit that outstrips the costs of the distortion. Although it is difficult to calculate the returns to education, available estimates suggest that the returns to educational achievement—as measured by test scores—can be large (Hanushek and Woessmann, 2008). As a result, an incentives system that produces substantial true gains in education could produce a net benefit even after accounting for the costs of distortion. However, in many settings, calculations of the benefits of test-based accountability are likely to be grossly exaggerated if they take test score gains at face value and ignore score inflation and the invisible effects of deemphasizing important skills that are not included on the tests. When real learning gains are small, costs may exceed benefits even when test scores have increased substantially.

Considering the effect of incentives on different people, it is important to recognize the fact that some individuals are harmed by an incentives policy does not automatically imply that such a policy should not be used. Test-based incentives for students may cause some students to achieve more and others to drop out, even with extra support and remediation. Test-based incentives for teachers may cause some teachers to become more effective and others to leave the profession. Test-based incentives for schools may cause some to focus on the full curriculum and others to focus on test preparation. In each case, it clearly matters how many people are affected in positive and negative ways and how large those effects are.

PSYCHOLOGICAL RESULTS AND ISSUES

As in economics, psychology has a long-standing appreciation of the importance of incentives in motivating behavior—going back to the beginning of the discipline—with research over the past few decades showing the complexity of the relationship between incentives and behavior. This research has led to the counterintuitive finding that under some circumstances incentives actually *reduce* the behavior that is being rewarded rather than increase it.

The counterintuitive result has shown up in experiments that provide an explicit incentive that takes the place of preexisting internal motivation by rewarding people for behavior they would have engaged in anyway without the incentives. For instance, Deci (1971) found that when college students were paid to perform interesting cube puzzles, they were less likely to perform the puzzle on their own during a free-choice period. Similarly, when nursery school children were offered a "good player award" for drawing a picture, they were less likely to draw when they were back in their regular classrooms (Lepper, Greene, and Nisbett, 1973). Once explicitly rewarded for a particular behavior, people tend to stop that behavior when the reward is discontinued. A number of other early studies showed that use of an external reward to motivate people to do something they would have done anyway can have detrimental effects on the quality and creativity of performance, as well as on subsequent motivation to perform the activity (Lepper and Greene, 1978).

The finding that external rewards can undermine internal motivation was initially very controversial, seeming to contradict both conventional wisdom and a wide body of experimental research in psychology. Over a decade, a succession of meta-analyses both supported (Rummel and Feinberg, 1988; Tang and Hall, 1995; Wiersma, 1992) and contested (Cameron and Pierce, 1994) that finding. These were followed by a new meta-analysis that provided a more complete and nuanced review of the contrasting conditions in the literature (Deci, Koestner, and Ryan, 1999). The new meta-analysis considered 128 studies published from 1971 to 1999, including each of the studies addressed by Cameron and Pierce (1994); this study showed clearly that tangible rewards do significantly and substantially undermine internal motivation.

Other research at the intersection of psychology and economics has shown that the way people perceive consequences and the way they decide between options with different consequences can be strongly affected by the way the different options are framed (see, e.g., Ariely, 2008; Rabin, 1998). For example, options framed as losses are perceived differently than the same options framed as gains. Similarly, people may reject options that are objectively better if the options are framed in a way that makes them seem unfair. A number of researchers have attempted to reconcile these psychological findings with the more standard view from economics that people choose according to the objective benefits of the different options, without reference to how those benefits are described (e.g., Fehr and Falk, 2002; Frey and Jegen, 2001).

In the rest of this section, we look in more detail at the specific circumstances that produce the negative effect of rewards on internal motivation, and on the research that has focused on learning and educational settings. We do so in three areas:

1. internal and external motivation,
2. the motivation to learn, and
3. incentives and public service work.

Internal and External Motivation

Deci and Ryan (1985) synthesized the large body of experimental work on human motivation in a theory that provides a framework for understanding the varying effects of external rewards. In this theory, internal motivation derives from a basic human need for self-determination that involves being able to make choices and manage the interaction between oneself and one's environment. When self-determined, a person will "engage in an activity with a full sense of wanting, choosing, and personal endorsement" (Deci, 1992, p. 44). The need for self-determination involves needs for autonomy, competence, and relatedness, each of which can be affected by external rewards.

Autonomy refers to the extent that people do something of their own choosing, both in and out of the context of external pressures. For example, one student may do homework simply to avoid punishment from his parents. Another student may do homework because she believes, despite a lack of interest in the topic, that it may be useful to her career. Both students are doing things that they would not do out of interest, so both are externally motivated. Yet the behavior of the second student entails more of an element of choice rather than simple compliance, and therefore she is exercising a certain degree of autonomy. The student has identified and understood the importance of the behavior and has internalized and assimilated it. In this respect, the student's behavior shares many characteristics with behavior that is internally motivated.

It is creating this type of "buy-in" that is such a challenge for educators and employers. It can be fostered by giving a student a sense of relatedness, which is a sense of belonging with the school (or other institution, person, or family) and sharing and accepting its mission or goal. Competence is another key factor—that is, the feeling on the part of a student that she understands the goal and has the skills to succeed.

This contrasts with the first student, who is simply complying with his parents but likely feels controlled, with little autonomy, which has a negative effect on internal motivation. The needs for autonomy, competence, and relatedness help to make sense of the effects of external rewards in different contexts.

One particularly interesting finding on the effects of external rewards relates to rewards for doing well or meeting a specified standard. The effects of such rewards have been shown to be mixed (Deci, Koestner, and Ryan, 1999): sometimes receiving a reward that signifies competence appears to enhance subsequent motivation, sometimes it seems to decrease subsequent motivation, and sometimes it seems to have no effect. The key seems to be that when rewards signifying competence are used in a way that seems very controlling to the person—so that it limits autonomy—the result tends to be negative. However, if a reward does not seem to be pressuring but instead simply signifies competence, it can have the intended positive effect. When people are told their performance is being evaluated, it is often experienced as controlling, and internal motivation may decrease even when positive evaluative information is subsequently provided (Harackiewicz, Abrahams, and Wageman, 1987).

The information provided by the reward can also be important. In situations in which higher performers receive higher rewards while lower performers receive lower rewards, the less-rewarded performers tend to interpret the shortfall as a signal not only that they did poorly this time, but also that they are unlikely to do well in the future. People who feel incompetent stop trying and become "demotivated." This effect has been found to be quite large (Deci, Koestner, and Ryan, 1999).

Rewards need not be tangible. The effects of verbal praise are also complex (Henderlong and Lepper, 2002). Verbal rewards are generally predicted to enhance internal motivation because they are informational, and they also feed a person's feelings of competence. However, not all praise has a positive effect. Several studies have shown that controlling positive feedback that seems to pressure the recipient ("good, you did just as you should") leads to less internal motivation than positive feedback that is purely informational ("you did well on that task") (Pittman et al., 1980; Ryan, 1982). One study found that verbal feedback that emphasizes performance relative to others tends to reduce internal motivation, whereas feedback centered on whether one has reached a certain level of performance on the task tends to increase interest in the task (Harackiewicz Abrahams, and Wageman, 1987).

The kinds of goals that are set also affect motivation. The highest level of effort occurs when the task is moderately difficult, and the lowest levels occur when the task is either very easy or very hard (Abramson et al., 1978; Atkinson, 1964; Csikszentmihalyi, 1990; Deci and Ryan, 1985).

When goals are set so high that people do not believe they can achieve them, the goals are demotivating and set the stage for feelings of helplessness, reduced effort, withdrawal, and lower self-esteem. Another factor is the specificity of the goals that are set: identifying specific, difficult goals leads to higher performance than does simply urging people to do their best (Locke and Latham, 2002). This occurs because do-your-best goals have no external referent and allow for a wide range of acceptable performance levels. The ideal goals provide optimal challenge: they encourage people to stretch themselves and are attainable with effort. Incentives can in turn affect the goals that people set for themselves: when people are given a choice of tasks that differ in terms of difficulty, they tend to choose relatively easy tasks if there is an external reward for successful completion, but they choose more challenging tasks in the absence of an external reward (Shapira, 1976).

The Motivation to Learn

Rewards-based incentive systems are commonly used in educational settings. For example, many teachers try to improve student performance by systematically rewarding students who follow classroom rules with praise, gold and silver stars, or tokens exchangeable for prizes.[4] Grades and honor rolls are intended to recognize excellence in achievement, but they may come to serve as external rewards to motivate students to work hard.

Incentives can backfire if they reduce the motivation that students have to learn. Young children have a natural propensity to learn that prompts exploration, curiosity, and a readiness to engage new material that frequently results in learning without the application of any external incentives. Given this propensity, why is the use of grades a standard part of the educational system? Part of the answer is that grades provide information to others (such as parents and college admissions officers) about how students have done, as well as information to the students themselves that they are learning the right things. Another part of the answer, of course, is that students are not always motivated to learn the things that may be useful or important for them to learn, so that the external signaling and motivation provided by grades can encourage students to learn skills and topics they might otherwise ignore. Sometimes the initial learning produced by external motivation will lead students to discover an interest in a new area that can lead to internal motivation for later learning.

---

[4]See, for example, the National Education Association's resources on classroom management at http://www.nea.org/classmanagement/archive.html [December 2010].

The key to using rewards in the classroom is to do so in a way that fosters autonomous motivation. As discussed above, autonomous motivation involves engaging students in a learning activity by helping them identify with and fully accept its importance for their own personal goals and values, even though the activity is not inherently interesting to them (at least initially) and therefore not internally motivating. An example would be a student who studies biology very hard in order to get excellent grades so she can go to medical school, because that is her personal goal. Autonomous motivation has been found to be a strong predictor of both conceptual learning and psychological well-being (Benware and Deci, 1984; Deci, Ryan and Williams, 1996; Grolnick and Ryan, 1987; Grolnick, Ryan, and Deci, 1991). Autonomous motivation has also been found to be associated with greater creativity on art activities at the elementary level (Koestner et al., 1984), less likelihood of dropping out for high school students (Vallerand et al., 1997), and a preference for challenges (Shapira, 1976).

Contemporary theories of motivation predict that tests and other forms of evaluation will best foster learning when they have informational significance. Evaluations would be expected to be most motivating when they provide relevant feedback in a noncontrolling way—that is, by providing individuals with specific feedback that points the way to becoming more effective or more competent, but without pressure or control. Motivation research suggests that when evaluations are experienced as controlling, they may produce temporary compliance, but they ultimately undermine internal motivation and commitment to the activity. And when evaluations convey incompetence to the individual, or when they are based on overly challenging standards that are perceived to be beyond the reach of the individuals, they are likely to reduce motivation and lead to a withdrawal of effort.

Both experimental and field studies have supported these predictions concerning the effects of evaluations on motivation (Ryan and Brown, 2005). For example, in one experiment at an elementary school (Grolnick and Ryan, 1987), students were given a reading comprehension task under three conditions: (1) they were told they would not be tested at all; (2) they were told they would be tested, but only to determine what kinds of ideas were learned, with no consequences for failure or success; and (3) they were told they would be tested and graded, and the grade would be delivered to their classroom teacher. The results showed that under the third condition—which represented a controlling use of evaluations—the students demonstrated short-term, rote memory but produced a significantly lower level of conceptual learning than the two noncontrolling conditions.

Classroom studies have shown that when teachers are oriented toward being controlling (for example, using evaluations and rewards), students are less internally motivated, less desirous of challenges in schools, and less confident in their skills (Deci et al., 1981; Ryan and Grolnick, 1986). What leads teachers to be controlling? They may become controlling when they themselves are pressured to get students to perform. In one study (Deci et al., 1982), participants were given the task of helping students learn a cognitive-perceptual task. The teachers all had the same set of problems to work with and were given the same preparation. However, one group of teachers was explicitly told that it was their job to make sure their students performed "up to high standards," while the other group received no such instruction. The participants who were pressured to produce high student achievement were more controlling and less supportive of students' autonomy. Specifically, they engaged in more lecturing, criticizing, praising, and directing—all techniques that have been shown to have a negative impact on students' interest in learning and their willingness to undertake difficult academic challenges. A subsequent study (Flink, Boggiano, and Barrett, 1990) examined this effect in the context of a newly introduced school-based curriculum for elementary students across several schools. As would be predicted by the prior work, the results showed that teachers pressed toward higher standards were more likely to engage in controlling instructional behaviors, and the more they did so, the more poorly the students actually performed on the objective tests.

Finally, there is evidence to suggest that focusing parents' concerns on performance outcomes will lead them, like teachers, to use pressuring motivational strategies that may backfire, leading to lower achievement over the long term (Grolnick, 2003; Grolnick et al., 2002). In contrast, parents who are supportive of their children's autonomy can help them to be more internally motivated (Grolnick, 2009).

Incentives and Public Service Work

Although most jobs include an external financial reward, many people enjoy work and do not do it only because they are paid. Organizational psychologists have found that people are most motivated in jobs that involve a wide variety of tasks, give them autonomy, provide good feedback, and encourage identification with the organization's mission (Griffin, 1991). The organization's mission may be particularly important to teachers and other people in public service who are motivated by the opportunity to contribute to society by such goals as educating children, caring for the elderly, or helping the unemployed (Burgess and Ratto, 2003; Heinrich and Marschke, 2010; Prendergast, 1999). One example of the commitment of teachers to the mission of educating children is the finding, from two surveys (Ingersoll, 2003, p. 179), that most teachers spend a substantial amount of their own money on curriculum materials and classroom supplies.

People in public service professions often view themselves as organizational stewards and may be motivated primarily by internal rewards, such as trust, autonomy, and job satisfaction, and the goals of their organization. The feeling of contributing to the public good may satisfy their personal needs and goals. In the field of public administration, research has found support for the importance of public service motivation (Heinrich and Marschke, 2010).

This motivation potentially has implications for the effectiveness of external incentives in public service occupations. Because of their underlying motivation, giving public service workers a financial incentive may be counterproductive, in that it signals that the relationship between the organization and the employee more closely resembles a market one, thus diluting effort and motivation (Burgess and Rato, 2003). Although there have been successful public-sector incentive programs—such as a Brazilian program that tied the pay of tax collectors to the number of tax evaders they apprehended (Kahn et al., 2001)—it is important that the incentives structure be aligned with the mission of the organization. Chapter 4 discusses the evidence related to providing performance pay for teachers.

CONCLUSIONS

The overarching message about incentives from research in economics, psychology, and related fields is that the details of incentive systems are critical to their success. Although there are many situations in which incentives work in a straightforward way, increasing the targeted behavior as intended, there are also many situations in which incentives fail to produce their desired effect because important details have not been taken into account.

Although the research in economics and psychology shares a high-level conclusion about the complexity of the link between incentives and behavior, the two fields point toward different considerations when one considers the research on the use of incentives in education. Work in economic theory analyzes the likely effect of incentives that are structured in different ways. These differences tend to be defined in concrete terms—who receives what consequence under what conditions. In contrast, much of the recent work in psychology about incentives analyzes subtleties in the different ways that incentives are framed and communicated.

When the committee looked at the ways that incentives have been used in education, this difference in the types of features considered by economics and psychology affected our ability to identify the relevant contrasts in existing educational research. In the large-scale applications of incentives that we review, we are able to note interesting and potentially important contrasts in the types of features suggested by economic theory—who gets what, when—but we are not able to note interesting contrasts in how the incentives are framed and communicated to the people they seek to influence. As a result, our synthesis of the basic research provides more detail about the findings from economic theory because we are able to use that detail to guide our review of the research on applications of incentives in education (see Chapter 4).

As the research in economic theory discussed in this chapter shows, at least four key elements need to be carefully considered in designing incentive systems: who is targeted by the incentives, what performance measures are used, what consequences are used, and what support is provided.

Target In complex organizations, incentives can be designed for people in different positions who can affect outcomes in different ways. Although the effects of incentives will be transmitted informally through the organization, that transmission will likely be imperfect. It may be important to target direct incentives to the people who can make the changes needed to improve outcomes.

Performance Measures The performance measures used with incentives have to be aligned with the desired outcomes for the incentives to have their desired effect. In particular, the measures need to be chosen so that behavior that increases the measures also increases the desired outcomes.

Consequences The size and structure of the consequences provided by the incentives will affect how the incentives operate and should be designed to be appropriate to the situation.

Support Incentives will typically have different effects for different people who have different abilities to successfully reach the target that will provide a reward or avoid a sanction. Without resources in support of an organization's objectives, incentives can be discouraging to the very people they are often intended to help, particularly if those people do not have the capacity to be successful.

The literature in psychology is not inconsistent with the four elements above—and much early psychological research focused precisely on such structural features of incentives—but much recent work in psychology about incentives has focused on a different element that has proven to be important in many settings: how incentives are framed and communicated.

Framing and Communication In most organizations, the commitment people have to the organization's mission is a critical part of their motivation. Incentives need to be framed and communicated in ways that reinforce that commitment—rather than erode it—by emphasizing the information they provide on progress toward shared goals.

In the chapters that follow we look at the use of test-based incentives in education through the lens of these key elements, with the caveat that we are able to say nothing about interesting contrasts in how incentives have been framed and communicated.

The research in economic theory discussed in this chapter also raises two important points related to evaluating the success of incentive systems, nonincentivized performance measures for evaluation and weighing costs and benefits.

- *Nonincentivized performance measures for evaluation*: Incentives will often lead people to find ways to increase measured performance that do not also improve the desired outcomes. Because of the resulting distortion in the performance measures used with the incentives, it is usually necessary to find different performance measures—that are *not* being used in the incentives system—to use when evaluating how the incentive system is working.
- *Weighing costs and benefits*: Incentive systems will typically generate a mix of costs and benefits that must be weighed against each other to determine the net value of the system. The costs will include monetary costs associated with running the system itself, as well as nonmonetary costs, such as the negative reactions of people who are left out of rewards or sanctioned under the incentive rules.

Again, the literature in psychology is not inconsistent with these two points from economics about how incentive systems should be evaluated, but the focus of recent work on psychology related to incentives speaks more directly to another point, changes in disposition.

- *Changes in dispositions*: In addition to evaluating the changes in a set of defined objective outcomes, it is important to consider the way incentive systems affect people's dispositions. No matter how broadly an incentives system is designed, in most situations we are likely to care about a broader range of outcomes than could be measured by available performance measures and rewarded by feasible incentive systems. With respect to these broader outcomes, it is important to know how incentives change the way people are disposed to act when they are not being directly affected by the incentives.

We consider these points further in Chapter 4 in the context of our discussion about the use of test-based incentives in education, with the caveat that we are able to say little about how these incentives have changed people's dispositions to act when they are not being directly affected by the incentives.

3

Tests as Performance Measures

As Chapter 2 discusses, the performance measures that are used with incentives are critically important in determining how incentives operate. Specifically, performance measures need to be aligned with the desired outcomes so that behavior that increases the measures also increases the desired outcomes. In this chapter we look at the use of tests as performance measures for incentive systems in education.

We have noted above that tests fall short as a complete measure of desired educational outcomes. Most obviously, the typical tests of academic subjects that are used in test-based accountability provide direct measures of performance only in the tested subjects and grade levels. In addition, less tangible characteristics—such as curiosity, persistence, collaboration, or socialization—are not tested. Nor are subsequent achievements, such as success in work, civic, or personal life, which are examples of the long-term outcomes that education aims to improve.

In this chapter, we turn to some important limits about tests that are not obvious—specifically, the ways they fall short in providing a direct measure of performance even in the tested subjects and grades. We begin by looking at an essential characteristic of tests themselves and then turn to review the ways that test results can be turned into performance measures that can be used with incentives. Finally, we look at the use of multiple measures in incentive systems in which there is an attempt to overcome the limitations of any single measure by using a set of complementary measures.

TESTS AS ESTIMATES FROM A SUBSET OF A DOMAIN

Although large-scale tests can provide a relatively objective and efficient way to gauge the most valued aspects of student achievement, they are neither perfect nor comprehensive measures. Many policy makers in education are familiar with the concept of test reliability and understand that the test score for an individual is measured with uncertainty. Test scores will typically differ from one occasion to another even when there has been no change in a test taker's proficiency because of chance differences in the interaction of the test questions, the test taker, and the testing context. Researchers think of these fluctuations as measurement error and so treat test results as estimates of test takers' "true scores" and not as "the truth" in an absolute sense.

In addition, tests are estimates in another way that has important implications for the way they function when used as performance measures with incentives: they cover only a subset of the content domain that is being tested. There are four key stages of selection and sampling that occur when a large-scale testing program is created to test a particular subject area. Each stage narrows the range of material that the test covers (Koretz, 2002; Popham, 2000). First, the domain to be tested, when specifically defined, is typically only part of what might be reasonable to assess. For example, there needs to be a decision about whether the material to be tested in each grade and subject should include only material currently taught in most schools in the state or whether it should include material that people think *should* be taught in each grade and subject.

Second, the test maker crafts a framework that lists the content and skills to be tested. For example, if history questions are to be part of the eighth grade test, they might ask about names and the sequence of events or they might ask students to relate such facts to abstractions, such as rights and democracy. These decisions are partly influenced by practical constraints. Some aspects of learning are more difficult or costly to assess using standardized measures than others. In reading, for example, students' general understanding of the main topic of a text is typically more straightforward to assess than the extent to which a student has formed connections among parts of the text or applied the text to other texts or to real-world situations.

Third, the test maker develops specifications that dictate how many test questions of certain types will constitute a test form. Such a document describes the mix of item formats (such as multiple choice or short answer), the distribution of test questions across different content and skill areas (such as the number of test questions that will assess decimal numbers or percentages), and whether additional tools will be allowed (such as calculators or computers).

Fourth, specific test items (questions) are created to meet the test specifications. After a set of test items of the correct types are created, the items are pilot-tested with students to see whether they are at the appropriate level of difficulty and are technically sound in other ways. On the basis of the results of the pilot test and expert reviews, the best test items are selected to be used on the final test. It is generally more difficult to design items at higher levels of cognitive complexity and to have such items survive pilot testing.

As a result of these necessary decisions about how to focus the content and the types of questions, the resulting test will measure only a subset of the domain being tested. Some material in the domain will be reflected in the test and other material in the domain will not. If one imagines the full range of material that might be appropriate to test for a particular subject—such as eighth grade mathematics as it is taught in a particular state—then the resulting test might include questions that reflect, for example, only three-quarters of that material. The rest of the material—in this hypothetical example, the remaining quarter of the subject that is excluded—would simply not be measured by the test, and this missing segment would typically be the portion of the curriculum that deals with higher levels of cognitive functioning and application of knowledge and skills.

Score Inflation

Although the example of a test covering only three-quarters of a domain is hypothetical, it provides a useful way to think about what can happen if instruction shifts to focus on test preparation in response to test-based incentives. If teachers move from covering the full range of material in eighth grade mathematics to focusing specifically on the portion of the content standards included on the test, it is possible for test scores to increase while learning in the untested portions of the subject stays the same or even declines. That is, test preparation may improve learning of the three-quarters of the domain that is included on the test by increasing instruction time on that material, but that increase will occur by reducing instruction time on the remaining one-quarter of the material. The likely outcome is that performance on the untested material will show less improvement or decrease, but this difference will be invisible because the material is not covered by the test.

To this point, we have discussed problems with tests as accountability measures even when best practices are followed. In addition, now that tests are being widely used for high-stakes accountability, inappropriate forms of test preparation are becoming more widespread and problematic (Hamilton et al., 2007). Test results may become increasingly misleading as measures of achievement in a domain when instruction is focused too narrowly on the specific knowledge, skills, and test question formats that are likely to appear on the test. Overly narrow instruction might include such practices as drilling students on practice questions that were released from prior years' tests, focusing on the limited subset of skills, knowledge and question formats that are most likely to be tested, teaching test-taking tricks (such as the process of elimination for multiple-choice items or memorizing the two "common Pythagorean ratios" rather than learning the Pythagorean theorem), or teaching students to answer open-ended questions according to the test's scoring rubric. When scores increase on a test for which students have been "prepared" in these ways, it indicates only that students have learned to correctly answer the specific kinds of questions that are included on that particular test. It does not indicate that that students have also attained greater mastery of the broader domain that the test is intended to represent (Koretz, 2002).

Changing teaching in at least some classrooms is one goal of test-based incentives. Good test preparation is instruction that leads to students' mastery of the full domain of knowledge and skills that a test is intended to measure. This mastery will incidentally improve large-scale test scores, but it will also be reflected elsewhere, for example, on other tests and in the application of knowledge outside school.

It is an essential goal of education reform that instruction be tied to the full set of intended learning goals, not just the tested sample of knowledge, skills, and question formats. Bad or inappropriate test preparation is instruction that leads to test score gains without increasing students' mastery of the broader, intended domain, which can result from engaging in the types of inappropriate strategies discussed above. These practices are technically permissible and can even be appropriate to a limited degree, but they will not necessarily help students understand the material in a way that generalizes beyond the particular problems they have practiced. Mastering content taught in test-like formats has been shown not to generalize to mastery of the same content taught or tested in even slightly different ways (Koretz et al., 1991). In this kind of situation, test scores are likely to give an inflated picture of students' understanding of the broader domain.

If test score gains are meaningful, they must generalize to the intended domain, and if they do, they should also generalize to a considerable extent to other tests and nontest indicators of the same domain. For that reason, trends in performance on the National Assessment of Educational Progress (NAEP)—a broad assessment designed to reflect a national consensus about important elements of the tested domains—are frequently compared with trends on the tests that states use for accountability.

One study examined the extent to which the large performance gains shown on the Kentucky Instructional Results Information System (KIRIS), the state's high-stakes test, represented real improvements in student learning rather than inflation of scores (Koretz and Barron, 1998). The study found evidence of score inflation. Even though KIRIS was designed partially to reflect the frameworks of NAEP, very large and rapid KIRIS gains in fourth grade reading from 1992 to 1994 were not matched by gains in NAEP scores. Although large KIRIS gains in mathematics from 1992 to 1994 in the fourth and eighth grades were accompanied by gains in NAEP scores, Kentucky's NAEP gains were roughly one-fourth as large as the KIRIS gains and were typical of gains shown in other states. At the high school level, the large gains that students showed on KIRIS in mathematics and reading were not reflected in their scores on the American College Testing (ACT) college admissions tests.[1] A Texas study found similar evidence of score inflation (Klein et al., 2000).

In a recent comparison of state test and NAEP results between 2003 and 2007, the Center on Education Policy (2008) found that trends in reading and mathematics achievement on NAEP generally moved in the same positive direction as trends on state tests, although gains on NAEP tended to be smaller than those on state tests. The exception to the broad trend of rising scores on both assessments occurred in eighth grade reading, in which fewer states showed gains on NAEP than on state tests.

The average scores on state accountability tests tend to rise, sometimes dramatically, every year for the first 3 or 4 years of use and then level off (Linn, 2000). When an existing test is then replaced with a new test or test form, the scores on the new test rise while the scores on the old test fall. Linn surmised that these initial gains reflect growing familiarity with the specific format and content of the new test. This explanation was supported by a study in which students were retested with an old test 4 years after a new test had been introduced in a large district (Koretz et al., 1991): while students' performance on the new test had increased, their performance had dropped on the test no longer routinely used. This result showed that the initial gains on the new test were specific to that test and did not support a conclusion of improved learning in the subject matter domain. A number of other studies provide persuasive evidence that gains on high-stakes accountability tests do not always generalize to other assessments given at approximately the same time in the same subjects (Fuller et al., 2006; Ho and Haertel, 2006; Jacob, 2005, 2007; Klein et al., 2000; Koretz and Barron, 1998; Lee 2006; Linn and Dunbar, 1990).

There is also evidence that teachers themselves lack confidence in the meaningfulness of the score gains in their own schools. A survey of educators in Kentucky asked respondents how much each of seven factors had contributed to score gains in their schools (Koretz et al., 1996a).

---

[1] The two tests measure somewhat different constructs, but the overlap was sufficient that one would expect a substantial echo of the KIRIS trends in ACT data.

Over half of the teachers said that "increased familiarity with KIRIS [the state test]" and "work with practice tests and preparation materials" had contributed a great deal. In contrast, only 16 percent reported that "broad improvements in knowledge and skill" had contributed a great deal. Very similar results were found in Maryland (Koretz et al., 1996b).

Fundamentally, the score inflation that results from teaching to the test is a problem with attaching incentives to performance measures that do not fully reflect desired outcomes in a domain that is broader than the test. It is unreasonable to implement incentives with narrow tests and then criticize teachers for narrowing their instruction to match the tests. When incentives are used, the performance measures need to be broad enough to adequately align with desired outcomes. One route to doing this is to use multiple measures, which we discuss later on in the chapter. However, another important route to broadening the performance measures is to improve the tests themselves. Finally, given the inherent limits in the breadth that can be achieved on tests, it is important to evaluate test results for possible score inflation.[2]

Broadening Tests to Reflect the Domain of Interest

A test will not provide good information about students' learning, in an accountability context when incentives have been attached to the results, unless it samples well—both in terms of breadth and depth—from the content that students have studied and asks questions in a variety of ways to make sure that students' performance covers the domain. That is: Can a test's results be generalized beyond that test?

In current practice, this concern is addressed in part by examining the alignment of tests with content and performance standards. However, it is not enough to have the limited alignment obtained when test publishers show that all of their multiple-choice items can be matched somewhere within the categories of a state's content standards (Shepard, 2003). Rather, what is needed is a more complete and substantive type of alignment "that occurs when the tasks, problems, and projects in which students are engaged represent the range and depth of what we say we want students to understand and be able to do. Perhaps a better word than alignment would be *embodiment*" (Shepard, 2003, p. 123). Shepard goes on to warn that "when the conception of curriculum represented by a state's large-scale assessment is at odds with content standards and curricular goals, then the ill effects of teaching to the external, high-stakes

---

[2]Such monitoring can be done by looking at low-stakes tests that are not attached to the incentives. In addition, see the work by Koretz and Béguin (2010) on possibilities for designing tests that include a component to self-monitor for score inflation.

test, especially curriculum distortion and nongeneralizable test score gains, will be exaggerated" (p. 124). To the extent feasible, it is important to broaden the range of material included on tests to better reflect the full range of what we expect students to know and be able to do.

In addition to broadening the range of material included on tests to better reflect the content standards they are intended to measure, it is also important to broaden the questions that are used to assess performance. Currently, one can find many unnecessary recurrences in the characteristics of many tests—unneeded similarities in content, format, other aspects of presentation, and aspects of the responses demanded (Koretz, 2008a). In some cases, one can find items that are near clones of items used in previous years, with only minor details changed. These unnecessary recurrences provide opportunities for coaching, and, indeed, test preparation materials often focus on them. Reducing these recurrences would make it harder to focus instructional time on tested details and thereby reduce score inflation when incentives are attached to the tests.

CONSTRUCTING INDICATORS FROM TEST RESULTS

Incentives are rarely attached directly to individual test scores; rather, they are usually attached to an indicator that summarizes those scores in some way. The indicators that are constructed from test scores have a crucial role in determining how the incentives operate. Different indicators created from the same test can produce dramatically different incentives.

A choice of indicator is fundamentally a choice about what a policy maker values and what pressures the policy maker wants to create by the incentives of test-based accountability. Is the goal to affect particular students, such as those who are high achievers, low achievers, or English learners? Is the only goal to ensure that everyone reaches some minimum performance level, or should progress below the minimum that fails to reach the minimum as well as progress above the minimum also be encouraged? It can be difficult to talk about the trade-offs that these questions imply, but the indicators used in test-based accountability implicitly include decisions about how such tradeoffs have been made.

For example, two commonly used ways of constructing indicators from test scores—mean scores and minimum performance levels—result in dramatically different incentives. A mean score places value on scores at all levels of achievement: every student who improves raises the mean and every student who declines lowers the mean. An incentive attached to a mean score will focus efforts on the scores of students at any achievement level whose scores can be increased. In contrast, a performance standard for a specific minimum level of achievement focuses attention on the scores near the cut score that represents the standard. When a standard that defines a minimum performance level is set, efforts are focused on raising the performance of students below the standard up to that level, while keeping students just above it from falling below it. An incentive attached to an indicator based on a minimum performance level will focus instruction on students believed to be near the standard; there is no incentive to improve the performance of students who are already well above the standard or who are far below it.

Research has demonstrated the effect that incentives based on performance standards can have in focusing attention on students who are near the standard. In a study that analyzed test scores before and after the introduction of Chicago's own accountability program in 1996, and before and after the introduction of the No Child Left Behind (NCLB) Act requirements in 2002 (Neal and Schanzenbach, 2010), the greatest gains were shown by students in the middle deciles, particularly the third and fourth. Little or no gain was shown in the top decile, and the bottom two deciles showed no improvement or even a decline. A similar pattern was found in Texas during the 1990s (Reback, 2008): "marginal" students, meaning those on the cusp of passing or failing a state exam used to judge the quality of schools, showed the greatest improvements because the accountability system provided strong incentives for teachers to focus on them. Two other studies (Booher-Jennings, 2005; Hamilton et al., 2007) also found that teachers focused their efforts on students near the proficiency cut score; teachers even reported being concerned about the consequences of doing so for the instruction of high- and low-achieving students.

Indicators based on performance standards were adopted to give more interpretable summaries to policy makers and the public of how groups of students are performing. There is some question whether the use of performance standards actually accomplishes this goal of greater interpretability. The simple performance labels that are shared across many tests—basic, proficient, and advanced—mask substantial variation within the categories. The reason for this variation is that standard-setting is a judgmental process that can be affected by the particular process used, the panelists who implement the process, and the political pressures that may lead to adjustments for the final levels. Different standard-setting methods often produce dramatically different results, as do different groups of panelists (Buckendahl et al., 2002; Jaeger et al., 1980; Linn, 2003; Shepard, 1993). Despite improvements in standard setting methods over time, performance standards vary greatly in rigor across the states (McLaughlin et al., 2008). One prominent researcher concluded that this variability is so great as to render characterizations such as "proficient" meaningless—despite the rhetorical power of such terms (Linn, 2003). In any case, it is important to realize that the use of performance standards has additional implications when incentives are attached to indicators that are based on those performance standards.

Another basic difference in types of indicators is the contrast between indicators that look at the levels of test scores and indicators that look at changes in those levels. There are several different ways of constructing indicators that look at test score changes: cohort-to-cohort changes, growth models, and value-added models.

Cohort-to-Cohort Changes Some indicators of change look at the test scores of successive cohorts of students in a particular grade to see if the performance of the students in that grade is improving over time. NCLB includes an indicator based on this kind of cohort-to-cohort change in its "safe harbor" provision, which gives credit to schools that have sufficiently improved the percentage of students meeting the proficient performance standard in successive years, even if the percentage does not yet meet the state's target for that year (Center on Education Policy, 2003).

Growth Models Some indicators of change look at the growth paths of individual students using longitudinal data that has multiple test scores for each student over time (see, e.g., Raudenbush, 2004). An indicator based on growth can adjust for the point at which students start in each grade and focus on how much they are progressing in that year. Growth models are technically challenging, both because there are difficulties in linking scores from year to year (especially when students change schools), though many states are making substantial progress, and because the models may require tests that are linked from grade to grade, which is difficult to do (Doran and Cohen, 2005; Michaelides and Haertel, 2004). Researchers have proposed an approach to modeling growth that would structure both instruction and tests around "learning progressions" that describe learning in terms of conceptual milestones in each subject (National Research Council, 2006b), but such an approach is not yet common.

Value-Added Models There has been widespread interest in a special type of growth model that attempts to control statistically for differences across students to make it possible to quantify the portions of student growth that are due to schools or teachers. The appeal of indicators based on value-added models is the promise that they could be used to fairly compare the effectiveness of different schools and teachers, despite the substantial differences in the types of students at different schools and the factors that determine how students are assigned to teachers and schools. This is an active area of research, but the extent to which value-added models can realize their promise has not yet been determined (see, e.g., Braun, 2005; National Research Council, 2010).

These different ways for deriving indicators from changes in test scores focus on different questions and so can be used to provide different incentives when consequences are attached to the indicators. Cohort-to-cohort change indicators look at the change in successive cohorts and may be especially useful during periods of reform when schools and teachers are making substantial changes over a short period of time. In periods when the education system is relatively stable, there is no reason to expect cohort-to-cohort indicators to show any change. Growth indicators look at changes for individual students and provide a way of isolating the learning that occurs in a given year. Because one always expect students to be learning—whether there is education reform or not—growth models need to provide some sort of target to indicate what level of annual change is appropriate. Indicators of growth based on learning progressions offer a way to do this that is tied to the curriculum in a meaningful way, but the necessary curricula and tests for this approach have not yet been developed. Finally, indicators based on value added expand the focus beyond student learning to the contributions of their teachers or schools to learning, with the attempt to identify the portion of learning that can be attributed to a teacher or school. As with growth models in general, value-added models have no natural metric that defines how much value added is appropriate or to be expected. These models have been used to look at the distribution of results for different teachers and schools to identify those that are apparently more effective or less effective in raising test scores, as well as possible mechanisms for increasing effectiveness.

We also note the use of subgroup indicators, which have been an important part of the test-based accountability structure of NCLB. If there is concern that group measures may systematically mask the performance of different subgroups, then it is possible to calculate an indicator using the test scores of different subgroups of students rather than the test scores for the entire student population. Attaching incentives to indicators of test results for different subgroups focuses attention to how each of those subgroups is doing.

In summary, different indicators constructed from the same test can provide very different types of information and very different pressures for change when incentives are attached to them. When choosing an indicator, it is necessary for policy makers to think carefully about the changes they want to bring about, the actions that would bring about those changes, and the people who could perform those actions. The answers to these questions must guide the aggregation of students' scores into indicators so that the indicators highlight useful information that can help bring about the desired changes.

Each type of indicator also brings its own technical challenges, which may limit its ability to provide information that is fair, reliable, and valid. It is important to address these technical issues, and we have mentioned some of them briefly in our discussion. However, the message from our review of the research—an assessment of the big picture about the use of test-based incentives—is that different indicators result in very different incentives. Consequently, it is important for policy makers to fully consider possible indicators when they are designing a system of test-based accountability.

MULTIPLE MEASURES

The tests that are typically used to measure performance in education fall short of providing a complete measure of desired educational outcomes in many ways. In addition, the indicators constructed from tests highlight particular types of information. Given the broad outcomes people want and expect for education, the necessarily limited coverage of tests, and the ways that indicators constructed from tests focus on particular types of information, it is prudent to consider designing an incentives system that uses multiple performance measures.

One of the basic research findings detailed in Chapter 2 is the importance of aligning performance measures with desired outcomes. As we note in that chapter, incentive systems in other sectors tend to evolve toward using increasing numbers of performance measures as experience with the limitations of particular performance measures accumulates. This evolution can be viewed as a search for a set of performance measures that better covers the full range of desired outcomes and also monitors behavior that merely inflates the measured performance without actually improving outcomes. In this section we discuss the use of multiple performance measures in education.

Professional standards for educational testing and guidelines for using tests emphasize that important decisions should not be made on the basis of a single test score and that other relevant information should be taken into account (American Educational Research Association, American Psychological Association, and National Council on Measurement in Education, 1999; National Research Council, 1999). Adding information about student performance from other sources can enhance the validity and reliability of decisions. This standard was originally conceived with individual students in mind, cognizant of the fact that tests are only samples of what students know and can do. For example, when a student fails a high school exit exam, taking into account other test scores or samples of the student's work can guard against denying a diploma to someone who really has mastered the requisite material.

As the consequences of testing have become more serious for entire schools, education stakeholders are increasingly advocating the use of multiple measures for school accountability to help guard against wrongly identifying schools as failing or needing intervention. Adopting appropriate multiple measures is a design choice that satisfies professional standards and can offer a better representation of the full range of educational goals. Give the context of our focus on incentives, we are particularly interested in the possibility that a set of multiple measures may better reflect education goals and so can provide better incentives when consequences are attached to those measures.

"*Multiple measures*" is often used loosely and can refer to many different things. Sometimes it is used to mean multiple opportunities with the same measure: for example, in many states, students are allowed to retake the high school exit exam until they pass. In our discussion here, we specifically exclude a discussion of the interpretation of multiple measures that focuses on multiple opportunities to take the same test because that does not provide a way to broaden the performance measure to better reflect our goals. Rather, we focus on two other meanings of the term. One is the use of more than one indicator of a student's performance in one subject area, such as by using both standardized test scores and teachers' judgments to determine a student's level of mathematics achievement. The second meaning is assessing student achievement in multiple subjects, such as reading, writing, mathematics, and science, and combining indicators across domains. In both kinds of multiple measures, indicators can be combined in a conjunctive or compensatory fashion, each of which has implications when consequences are attached, as discussed below.

Conjunctive Models

Conjunctive models combine indicators but do not allow high performance on one measure to compensate for low performance on another. For example, NCLB uses a conjunctive or multiple-hurdle model. In order to make adequate yearly progress, a school must meet each of a number of conditions. The first is that 95 percent of students in each numerically significant subgroup must be tested. Then, all students, as well as all subgroups, must meet targets for percentage proficient. In addition, there are targets for attendance and graduation rates. This combination of measures is used to determine whether schools are making adequately yearly progress, with consequences if they are not. The consequences attached to this conjunctive system of measures sends the message that each indicator is important and schools are expected to meet each target. The result is that there is only one way to pass—to meet all of the requirements—and many ways to fail. For example, with NCLB, a school may have excellent test scores, but a shortfall in attendance would still cause the school to fail to make adequate yearly progress (Linn, 2007). With multiple ways to fail, the consequences in this system focus attention on the areas that are in danger of not meeting their targets.

Compensatory Models

In contrast to conjunctive models, compensatory models combine multiple indicators so that a low score in one area can be offset by a high score in another. This produces an overall picture of whether performance targets are being achieved, across the range of areas, but it does not require that each of the individual targets is achieved. Attaching consequences to a system of multiple measures using a compensatory model provides incentives to improve overall performance; the consequences in this system focus attention on the areas where there are the most opportunities for improvement, not areas that are most in danger of failing to meet their individual targets, because there are no individual targets. Compensatory incentives are appropriate in cases where policy makers want to ensure overall performance levels across a number of areas but not where they have individual targets for each of those areas that they view as critical.

In Ohio, for example, the system involves four indicators that are combined in a compensatory way to classify its districts and schools into five categories of performance. The four indicators are (1) the performance indicators for each grade and subject area (reading, writing, mathematics, science, and social studies); (2) a performance index that is a composite score based on all tested grades and subjects, weighted so that scores above proficient count more than those below proficient; (3) a growth calculation; and (4) adequate yearly progress under NCLB. Each indicator uses scores from the statewide testing program, and two of the indicators also consider attendance and graduation rates. The way the four different indicators complement each other to produce an aggregate measure has been described by one expert (Chester, 2005) as better than any single measure in capturing the varied outcomes that the state wants to monitor and encourage. For example, rather than viewing NCLB's measure of adequate yearly progress as a substitute for the state's entire system, Ohio understood that that measure provides crucial monitoring of subgroup performance that had previously been lacking in their system. Thus the adequate yearly progress indicator provides important additional information on the overall performance of the schools in the states, even though it fails to capture crucial information—about other subject areas, different levels of performance, and growth—that the other indicators in the system provide.

In cases where compensatory systems bring together different independent measures, they can have greater reliability than conjunctive systems in a statistical sense because information about the overall performance accumulates across indicators, and the random fluctuations that affect any single indicator tend to offset each other; a chance positive on one indicator can be offset by an equally chance negative on another, but information about performance is present in all indicators (Chester, 2005; Linn, 2007).

Compensatory systems can combine indicators either in a single subject area or across subject areas. Each version can be appropriate for some objectives and inappropriate for others.

The structure of high school exit exams in many states provides an example of the use of compensatory measures within a single subject area. Although people commonly think of high school exit exam requirements as requiring students to pass a single test, the actual requirement in many states involves additional routes to meeting the target. These multiple routes effectively create a compensatory system of multiple measures. In 2006, 16 of the 25 states with exit exams had policies in place for an alternate route to a diploma for students who could not pass the exams, yet had adequate attendance records and grades (Center on Education Policy, 2006b). For example, in a number of states students can use course grades, a collection of classroom work, or the results from a different test in the subject—such as an AP test—to make up for a failure to pass a subject on the state's high school exam. In states that allow these multiple routes, the high school exit exam requirement provides an overall incentive to meet the requirement but not to pass the test itself.

Similarly, there are examples of incentive systems that use compensatory models across subject areas. For example, at the individual level, Maryland's high school exit exam uses an overall score that combines results for different subjects (Center on Education Policy, 2005). At the state level, California's accountability program uses an academic performance index that combines indicators from four different tests: the state's standards-referenced test, a norm-referenced test, an alternate test, and the state's high school exit exam. The tested subjects are English, mathematics, history/social science, and science. The indicators are weighted on a scale that was determined by the state board of education and combined to give a final metaindicator of school performance (California Department of Education, 2011).

The essential principle in using a compensatory system of multiple measures is that attaching consequences to an overall compensatory index focuses the incentives at an overall level that uses a broader performance measure than any one measure alone. If the compensatory system is used for multiple indicators within a single subject area, then incentives will focus attention more broadly across the full range of the subject than a single test would. If the compensatory system is used for multiple indicators across subject areas, then incentives will focus attention across the full range of subject areas. In both cases, there are no targets for the individual measures—which means no targets on the individual tests when compensatory measures are used within a single subject area and no targets on the individual subjects when compensatory measures are used across subject areas. Attaching incentives to a compensatory system of multiple measures within a subject area may be appropriate for a subject area that is critical where there is concern about the necessarily limited coverage of each of the available measures. Attaching incentives to a compensatory system of multiple measures across subject areas may be appropriate where there is more concern about tracking overall performance and less concern about the relative performance in particular subject areas.

An Alternative Approach to Multiple Measures: Using Test Scores as a Trigger

Another possible approach is to use large-scale test scores as a trigger for a more in-depth evaluation, as proposed by Linn (2008). Under such a system, teachers or schools with low scores on standardized tests would not be subject to automatic sanctions. Instead, the results of standardized tests would be used as descriptive information in order to identify schools that may need a review of their organizational and instructional practices. With such identification, the appropriate authority would begin an intensive investigation to determine whether the poor performance was reflected in other measures, possibly including subjective measures.

One way of thinking about the trigger approach is that it effectively institutes a system of multiple measures in stages, incorporating additional measures of school performance only when the test score measures indicate a likelihood that there is a problem. The approach trades off greater reliability and validity of a system of multiple measures applied to all schools for a more detailed inspection carried out for those schools identified as possibly in trouble. In addition, the approach combines the step of obtaining additional information with the opportunity to provide initial recommendations for improvement, if they seem to be warranted.

Variations of this approach are already being used in some places (see Archer, 2006; McDonnell, 2008). For example, in Britain, teams of inspectors visit schools periodically to judge the quality of their leadership and ability to make improvements. The inspectors draw on test scores, school self-evaluations, and input from parents, teachers, and students and then issue a report on various aspects of the school's performance.

4

Evidence on the Use of
Test-Based Incentives

In Chapters 2 and 3, we discuss theory and research on incentives with brief references to tests, and testing with brief references to incentives. In this chapter we delve more fully into the intersection of tests and incentives with the goal of providing an interpretive review of different types of incentives in education in light of the basic research findings about how incentives operate and how they should be evaluated. We focus on rigorous studies that can provide guidance to policy makers about the effects of test-based incentives in education. Although our review does not cover all the available research about the use of test-based incentives in education, we have attempted to include all prominent studies from the past few years that satisfy the criteria we outline below.

In our descriptions of the structure of the test-based incentive programs, we provide information about the key elements that should be considered in designing incentive systems (see Chapter 2): who receives incentives (the targets of the incentive), what performance measures are used, what consequences are attached, and whether supports for improvement are provided. Unfortunately, the available program information often fails to adequately address these elements, which limits our ability to draw inferences about how they affect the outcomes.

In describing evidence about the effects of the incentive programs, we provide information about relevant outcomes other than the tests that are attached to the incentives in order to reduce the likelihood that our conclusions are biased by any distortion that the incentives may cause. We also offer information about changes on high-stakes tests, if it is available, but our focus is on evidence from other measures of the same domain, including both the results of low-stakes tests and other outcomes, such as graduation.

Tables 4-1A, 4-1B, 4-2, and 4-3, presented at the end of the chapter, summarize the descriptive and outcome information discussed in the text below. The studies or groups of studies are referred to below and in the tables as examples; by number, and in some cases additional by letter designations. In both the text and tables, we divide the studies we analyzed into three categories that are familiar to education policy makers and researchers: school-level policies related to the No Child Left Behind (NCLB) Act and its predecessors; high school exit exams; and experiments with teachers and students that use rewards, such as performance pay. Note that the first two categories address policies rather than experiments and so involve larger numbers of students, teachers, and schools and longer implementation periods, but they also present greater difficulties in identifying appropriate comparison groups. NCLB, as the one federal policy discussed in our review, involves particularly difficult challenges in identifying a comparison group.

STUDIES INCLUDED AND FEATURES CONSIDERED

Criteria for Inclusion

Our literature review is limited to studies that allow us to draw causal conclusions about the overall effects of incentive policies and programs.[1] In some cases, programs were planned to include untreated control groups for comparison; in other cases, researchers have carefully documented how to make appropriate comparisons. Because our purpose is to draw causal conclusions about the overall effects of test-based incentives, we exclude several kinds of studies that do not permit such conclusions:

- studies that omit a comparison group, including the evaluations of NCLB carried out by the U.S. Department of Education (Stulich et al., 2007), the Center on Education Policy (2008), and the Northwest Evaluation Association (Cronin et al., 2005), in addition to various well-known earlier studies (e.g., Klein et al., 2000; Richards and Sheu, 1992);
- cross-sectional studies that compare results with and without incentive programs but with no controls for selection into the

---

[1]For literature reviews that cover a broader range of related studies, see Figlio and Loeb (2010) on school accountability, Podgursky and Springer (2006) on teacher performance pay, and Holme et al. (2010) on high school exit examinations.

incentive programs, including well-known studies of exit exams (e.g., Jacob, 2001) and teacher performance pay (e.g., Figlio and Kenny, 2007); and

- studies that focus on contrasting results for students, teachers, or schools that are immediately above or below the threshold for receiving the consequences of the incentive programs,[2] including well-known studies of exit exams (e.g., Martorell, 2004; Papay et al., 2010; Reardon et al., 2010) and school incentives (e.g., Ladd and Lauen, 2009; Reback, 2008; Rouse et al., 2007).

Finally, we exclude programs using incentives that are too new to have meaningful results (e.g., Kemple, 2011; Springer and Winters, 2009).[3] Particularly in the area of performance pay for teachers, there has been strong recent interest in developing new incentive programs, and we expect these will make important additions to the research base in the near future.[4]

Policy and Program Features and Outcomes Considered

The features related to the structure of the incentive programs that we selected for our analysis are derived from four of the five key elements that should be considered in designing incentive programs (see Chapter 2).

Target Our analysis primarily included studies with incentives that were given to schools, teachers, or students, though one case provides an example of incentives given to both students and parents. We coded performance pay programs for teachers as being received by teachers

---

[2]Such regression discontinuity studies provide interesting causal information about the effect of being above or below the threshold, but they do not provide information about the overall effect of implementing an incentives program.

[3]New York City has recently implemented a performance pay program for teachers in about 200 schools using random assignment of eligible schools (see Springer and Winters, 2009). An initial analysis showed small and negative effects of the program on the tests linked to the incentives, but none of the effects was statistically significant, and the initial analysis used tests that were given less than 3 months after the program was instituted. In addition, New York City's reform effort since mayoral control of the schools began in 2002 includes a schoolwide performance bonus plan that began in the 2007-2008 school year. Initial analysis suggests that scores on the tests attached to the incentives increased faster during the reform period than occurred in comparable urban districts in New York (Kemple, 2011).

[4]See, for example, the various reports on the Texas performance pay program available from the National Center on Performance Incentives (see http://www.performance incentives.org [June 2011]).

either individually or as a group (Teachers-I or Teachers-G), depending on whether the incentives were based on the performance of each teacher's own students or on the performance of all students in the school.

Performance Measures We used the limited information about the performance measures to code two different features related to the coverage of the measures across subjects and within subjects. For most of the incentive programs we reviewed, the performance measures included only tests, but we noted other measures if they were used. We coded the content coverage across subjects as either narrow or broad, depending on whether the tests included only a portion of the curriculum or most subjects. Usually programs with narrow coverage across subjects focused on language and mathematics tests. When the studies compared results across states where some states used performance measures with broad coverage across subjects and others used performance measures with narrow coverage across subjects, we coded the coverage across subjects as mixed. We also coded the content coverage of the performance measures within subjects as either narrow or broad, depending on whether the test and the performance indicator were sensitive to the full range of content and skill within the subject or to only a portion of the content and skill. For the tests, we looked for information that the tests covered higher-order thinking skills within the subject area. For the performance indicator, we looked for information that the indicator reflected gains across the entire distribution of performance, such as by using a score average or a measure of test score gains rather than a performance level. We coded the coverage of the performance measure within subjects as broad only if both the test and the performance indicator were sensitive to the full range of content and skill.[5]

Consequences With respect to the basic structure of the programs, we coded whether they were focused primarily on penalizing poor performance with sanctions or rewarding performance that meets or exceeds expectations. In the text, we also describe the nature of the consequences and any available information about their frequency, but we did not attempt to code the consequences as large or small because we lacked an objective way of making such a determination.

---

[5]It was often easier to obtain information from the studies about the breadth of the performance indicators than it was to obtain information about the breadth of the tests. Since we required both the test and the indicator to be broad in order to code a program as using a broad performance measure within subjects, we were able to code many programs as using a narrow performance measure within subjects by looking at the performance indicator alone, without needing to obtain information about the test.

Supports To see whether the incentives program takes account of the ability of people to influence their performance, we coded whether or not resources or supports were provided to aid in the attainment of performance goals as part of the incentives program.

Our coding of the incentives structure captures the types of contrasts reflected in the economics literature, but it does not reflect those in the psychology literature about the way that incentives are framed and communicated. In the experimental work discussed in Chapter 2, the contrast between different conditions sometimes involved subtle differences in wording. It is plausible that most of the incentive programs we discuss could have been presented in ways that were either more positive or more negative, depending on whether those in leadership positions characterized them as supporting a shared commitment to learning or as posing an additional burden in already difficult circumstances. Even the contrast between sanctions and rewards fails to measure the way incentives were communicated in a district, school or classroom, since a skillful leader could have described potential sanctions as reaffirming a shared commitment to learning, and an inept leader could have described potential rewards as an attempt to impose external control. In many situations, the contrast between emphasizing one message or the other is subtle—just as it was in the experiments discussed in Chapter 2. The lack of a good measure of the way incentives are framed and communicated is an important limitation in our description of the structure of the different incentive programs.

The features in Table 4-1B related to the outcomes of the incentive programs reflect the importance of providing outcome measures other than the tests that are attached to the incentives. In addition, we looked for information about whether the program effects were distributed across all content areas included in the program and whether they differed for the relatively low- or high-performing students. Our analysis included the following features:

- effect on high-stakes test: the effect of the incentives program on the tests that were attached to the incentives in the program;
- effect on low-stakes test: the effect on tests that were in the same subjects as the tests attached to the program's incentives but that were not themselves attached to those incentives;
- effect on other subject tests: the effect of the program on tests in subjects other than those that were attached to the program's incentives;
- effect on graduation or certification: the effects of the program on graduation or college-bound certification;

- effect on lower performing students: the statistically significant effects of the program for students in the lower half of the achievement distribution; and
- effect on higher performing students: the statistically significant effects of the program for students in the upper half of the achievement distribution.

In the tables, the outcomes columns summarize the outcomes as positive, negative, or not statistically significantly different from zero.[6] If a study provided multiple results, the discussion below and the table entries summarize the overall tendency of the outcomes; if the results diverged, the multiple outcomes are discussed and shown in order of prevalence.

As with our coding of the structural features of the incentive programs, our coding of the outcomes of the programs failed to capture the important outcome from the psychology literature related to changes in dispositions. In general, the studies we analyzed did not provide information about such outcomes; however, a few studies were exceptions to this finding, and for these studies we note their findings related to changes in dispositions in the text.

NCLB AND ITS PREDECESSORS

We identified causal studies related to three examples of school incentives that are in the NCLB mold. Two related to the overall adoption of school incentives across the United States: Example 1 reflects the initiatives in a number of individual states before NCLB, and Example 2 reflects the changes that came with NCLB. Example 3 is Chicago, for both the initial district-level incentives in the 1990s and the implementation of the succeeding NCLB incentives.

Examples 1 and 2: Nationwide School Incentives

A number of states instituted test-based incentives during the 1990s, with consequences for schools that anticipated the consequences that were implemented for all states in 2001 under NCLB (Dee and Jacob, 2007; Hanushek and Raymond, 2005). Under NCLB, schools that do not show adequate yearly progress face escalating consequences. The structure of NCLB defines consequences for schools that involve increasing levels of state intervention and support to bring about improvement. The initial

---

[6]We used the most lenient level of statistical significance provided in each study, generally $p < 0.10$ or $p < 0.05$.

requirements are to file improvement plans, make curriculum changes, and offer their students school choice or tutoring; if progress does not improve as specified, they are required to restructure in various ways. The consequences are based on state tests in reading and mathematics that use state-defined targets for student proficiency. During 2006-2009, the proportion of schools failing to show adequate yearly progress ranged from 29 to 35 percent (Center on Education Policy, 2010). There is mixed information about the implementation of the consequences prescribed under NCLB, with frequent focus on making curriculum and instructional changes, but fewer cases of implementing effective school choice or tutoring options that students use (Center on Education Policy, 2006a).

We treated the incentive programs adopted by many states in the 1990s as roughly similar to NCLB although there were many variations in the incentive structures in the states that may have affected results. For example, North Carolina's school incentives, which were implemented in 1996 and continued alongside NCLB after 2001, are based on test score gains rather than proficiency levels and so are targeted to a broad range of performance rather than a narrow range near the proficiency cut point. Under the two different performance criteria, there were different outcomes: schools facing sanctions under NCLB improved the test scores of lower performing students, while schools facing sanctions under the state program improved the test scores of both lower and higher performing students (Ladd and Lauen, 2009). Unfortunately, there were no studies available that would have allowed us to contrast the overall effect of state incentive programs predating NCLB by the committee's key elements in incentive structure.

We considered three studies that identified causal effects of school incentive policies by comparing changes in states that did and did not use those policies. The studies used the National Assessment of Educational Progress (NAEP) to measure achievement in reading and mathematics for fourth and eighth grade students. For the early period, we used a meta analysis of 14 studies that compared states that started test-based incentives before NCLB with states that did not (Lee, 2008). For the later period, we used two studies that each performed a complementary analysis that compared states that started using school incentives under NCLB to states that already had school incentives before NCLB (Dee and Jacob, 2009; Wong, Cook, and Steiner, 2009).

Example 1: Pre-NCLB Nationwide School Incentives

For the early period, the meta-analysis by Lee (2008) identified 14 studies that compared results across states with different test-based accountability policies. Most of the studies used longitudinal NAEP data from the 1990s to compare states with different levels of test-based school accountability policy.[7] The studies defined the policy contrasts in a variety of ways and used a variety of analytic strategies. Some of the studies focused on mathematics, and others looked at both mathematics and reading. Most of the studies looked at test results in grades 4 and 8. Across the 76 effect sizes that were calculated from the studies, the average effect size associated with a contrast between states with and without test-based accountability was 0.08 standard deviations (Lee, 2008, p. 625); 66 were positive, 2 were zero, and 8 were negative (pp. 631-638).[8] The study did not report how many of these effects were statistically significant. The meta-analysis did not find significant differences in effect sizes between school and student incentive policies (p. 616), between mathematics and reading (p. 619), between different grade levels (p. 619), or between different racial and ethnic groups (p. 621).

Example 2A: NCLB Nationwide School Incentives (Dee and Jacob)

For the NCLB period, Dee and Jacob (forthcoming) estimated that the imposition of the NCLB requirements in states that had not yet adopted school incentives increased achievement by 2007 in fourth grade mathematics by 7.2 points in the preferred model (Dee and Jacob, forthcoming, Table 3, Panel B). This increase corresponds to an effect size of 0.23 standard deviations. The effects on eighth grade mathematics and fourth grade reading were positive, and the effect on eighth grade reading was negative; none of these other effects was statistically significant.[9] The paper did not provide a formal test of the statistical significance of the subject or grade differences in the effect sizes. Over four combinations of

---

[7]Given this generalization, the multiple studies in Lee (2008) can be thought of as effectively providing multiple analyses of a single big experiment across states in the 1990s, using different ways of analyzing the available NAEP data. Note that four studies included in Lee (2008) do not fit the generalization in the text: two involve cross-sectional comparisons (Bishop et al., 2001; Lee, 1998) and two focus exclusively on high school exit requirements that are based on minimum competency testing rather than school accountability (Fredericksen, 1994; Jacob, 2001), with one (Jacob, 2001) using the National Education Longitudinal Study rather than NAEP.

[8]The effect sizes are calculated in Lee (2008) from information provided in the original papers. The figure reported in the text is for effect sizes calculated in terms of the standard deviation of student scores. Note that many of the effect sizes reported in the paper are based on the standard deviation of state scores and so are not comparable to the versions calculated in terms of the standard deviation of student scores.

[9]The study notes uncertainty about the reading estimates because the fourth grade data do not follow the linear trend that the statistical model assumes and because the eighth grade data include only two pre-NCLB observations. The results for eighth grade reading were reported only in an appendix.

subject and grade, the average effect size was 0.08 standard deviations.[10] The increase for fourth grade mathematics occurred for both lower and higher performing students (Table 5). Finally, a check for changes in NAEP science test scores showed no effect of NCLB in either fourth or eighth grade on a subject without incentives (Table C4, Panel B), with a small positive effect in grade 4 and a small negative effect in grade 8, neither of which was statistically significant.

Example 2B: NCLB Nationwide School Incentives, Public Schools (Wong, Cook, and Steiner)

Wong, Cook, and Steiner (2009) found similar results for the NCLB period for public schools, though with some differences in their approach. In addition to the contrast between states with and without school incentives before NCLB used by Dee and Jacob, they added a contrast between states with high and low standards. Although high standards did not appear to interact with incentives,[11] the results suggested that the separate effects of the two policies combined in grade 4 reading to produce a statistically significant change. Across three combinations of subject and grade, the average effect size associated with incentives was 0.12 (Wong, Cook, and Steiner, 2009, Table 14).[12] The effect size was statistically significant only for fourth grade mathematics (Table 13). The paper omitted eighth grade reading, the one test for which Dee and Jacob found negative effects.

---

[10]We computed the average from the coefficients on the "Total effect by 2007" line of Table 3 in Dee and Jacob (forthcoming) dividing each by the standard deviation of the scores for the different tests provided at the bottom of the table. The results for eighth grade reading were taken from the corresponding line of appendix Table C2. Despite the authors' uncertainty about the reading estimates (see fn. 9), our analysis included them in the overall average in order to provide the best available average of the effect of NCLB that reflects a balance across subjects and grades. When the subjects were considered separately, the average effect for mathematics was 0.17 standard deviations, and the average effect for reading was 0.00 standard deviations.

[11]In the case of fourth grade mathematics, in one specification there was an interaction effect of standards and incentives with borderline statistical significance that suggests that either high standards or incentives alone produced the same effect as the two policies together (Wong, Cook, and Steiner, 2009, Table 13).

[12]We averaged the effect sizes in the "Diff. in Total Δ (2007 or 2009) CA" line of Table 14 of Wong, Cook, and Steiner (2009).

Example 2C: NCLB Nationwide School Incentives, Public and Private Schools (Wong, Cook, and Steiner)

Wong, Cook, and Steiner (2009) also used a comparison between public and private (mostly Catholic) schools as a way to estimate the effects of NCLB, though Dee and Jacob rejected this approach because of the decline in Catholic school enrollment that occurred around the start of NCLB (because of the sex abuse scandal). In addition to comparing public and Catholic schools, the study also compared public and non-Catholic private schools. Over six combinations of subject, grade, and private school type, there was an average effect size of 0.22 standard deviations associated with the change in public school NAEP scores by 2007 or 2009.[13] Although all of the effect sizes were positive, the only one that was marginally significant was for fourth grade mathematics for Catholic private schools (Wong, Cook, and Steiner, 2009, Table 6).

Related Studies About School Incentives

There have been a number of studies of the instructional changes that have accompanied the implementation of school incentives (e.g., Center on Education Policy, 2007a; Hamilton et al., 2007; Rouse et al., 2007; Stecher, 2002; White and Rosenbaum, 2008). In general, these studies found shifts in instruction that were consistent with the performance measures that were attached to the incentives. Some of these changes were aimed at improving achievement broadly, such as increasing total instruction time, improving the alignment of instruction with standards, or adding professional development for teachers. Other changes were focused on the specific structure of the incentives system, such as shifting instruction to focus on aspects that count in the system and away from aspects that do not count: these changes involved an increased focus on tested subjects, on lower performing students at the threshold of attaining proficiency, and on material that closely mimics the tests. These findings about instructional shifts underline the necessity of evaluating the effect of incentives with information from low-stakes tests in the same subjects as the tests attached to incentives, on students at different performance levels, and on subjects not attached to incentives.

In addition to changes in instruction in the subject area, there is evidence of attempts to increase scores in ways that are completely unrelated to improving learning. The attempts included teaching test-taking skills, excluding low-performing students from tests, feeding students high-

---

[13]We averaged the effect sizes in the "Diff. in Total Δ (2007 or 2009)" lines of Table 7 of Wong, Cook, and Steiner (2009) for the "Public vs. Catholic (Main NAEP)" and "Public vs. Non-Catholic (Main NAEP)" sections of the table.

calorie meals on testing days, providing help to students during a test, and even changing student answers on tests after they were finished (e.g., Cullen and Reback, 2006; Figlio and Getzler, 2006; Figlio and Winicki, 2005; Jacob and Levitt, 2003; Stecher, 2002). The evidence about behaviors that were likely to distort test results again underlines the importance of evaluating the effects of incentives using measures of the same domain that are different than the results of the tests attached to the incentives. It is also important to note, however, that some of the changes that can distort high-stakes tests—such as a focus on the portions of the subject that are easy to test—can also distort low-stakes tests.

Example 3: Chicago School Incentives

The incentives that Chicago introduced in 1996 included sanctions for both schools and students (Jacob, 2005). The school sanctions involved the possibility of reconstituting schools with a high percentage of low-performing students. The student sanctions involved mandatory summer school and retention for students unable to pass exams in the third, sixth, and eighth grades. If students were unable to pass the exams after summer school, they had an additional opportunity to rejoin their class if they could pass the exams in January of the following year. During the first 3 years of the program, retention rates in these grades increased to 10-20 percent, far above the prior level of 1-2 percent (Jacob and Lefgren, 2009).

Jacob (2005) used longitudinal data for Chicago that included the period before the policy took effect and controls for both prior test trends and changes in student demographics. For the 4 years after the start of school incentives, scores on the high-stakes tests in the three grades had increased above predicted trends by about 0.2 standard deviations in reading and 0.3 standard deviations in mathematics (Jacob, 2005, Table 1). Similar results were obtained by comparing the change in Chicago's test score trends when incentives were introduced with the test score trends in other large, midwestern cities (Table 2). Looking across students, there were generally positive effects for both lower and higher performing students in mathematics; for reading, the effects occurred primarily for lower performing students (Table 3). In the lowest decile of students, however, there was some indication that incentives decreased performance. Neal and Schanzenbach (2010) obtained similar results on the distribution of effects across students.

Jacob (2005, Table 5) replicated a version of his analysis with data on low-stakes tests in reading and mathematics. The analysis showed an effect of about 0.2 standard deviations in both subjects 2 years after implementation, but only for the eighth grade; the effect on the low-stakes tests for the third and sixth grade was either negative or was small and not statistically significant. Over nine combinations of subject, grade, and model specification, the average effect size was 0.04. Five of the effects were statistically significant, three of them positive and two of them negative; for the four effects that were not statistically significant, two were positive and two were negative.[14] A direct contrast of the results in mathematics across the three grades showed an average effect size of 0.11 standard deviations on the test attached to the incentive, in comparison with an effect size of 0.04 standard deviations on the test not attached to the incentive. In both cases two of the three effects were statistically significant, but for the high-stakes test both of the significant effects were positive, and for the low-stakes test one was positive and the other was negative.[15]

Jacob (2005, Table 8) also looked at changes in low-stakes tests in science and social studies for students in the fourth and eighth grades, finding that scores in these subjects increased after incentives were introduced. Although the increase in test scores for science and social studies was smaller than for reading and mathematics and occurred primarily with higher performing students, it was positive and so does not suggest a tradeoff between the high-stakes and low-stakes subjects.

HIGH SCHOOL EXIT EXAMS

Use of exit exams has been growing over the past three decades and now includes 25 states and two-thirds of public high school students (Center on Education Policy, 2007b; Warren et al., 2006). There is important variation across states in the nature of the tests used, with general movement over time from minimum competency tests of basic skills below the high school level, to standards-based tests at the ninth and tenth grade levels, to end-of-course tests that are focused on the content of specific high school courses. Exit exams typically involve tests in multiple subjects, all of which must be passed, though many states provide alternate paths that can be substituted for a failure on one or more subject tests (Center on Education Policy, 2006b). States and districts provide a variety of remediation programs and materials for students, as well as assistance to teachers to help prepare students for the exams (Center on Education Policy, 2007b). We identified three causal studies across a large

---

[14]We averaged the estimates for the Illinois Goal Assessment Program (IGAP) test from Table 5 in Jacob (2005), using the models that included controls and prior trends. We did not use the models without controls and prior trends because the study used observational data that cannot support a causal interpretation.

[15]We averaged the estimates for the ITBS and IGAP tests, respectively, in Panel A of Table in Jacob (2005), using the models that included controls and prior trends.

number of states; they used the staggered implementation of exit exams to examine their effect on several different outcomes.

Example 4A: Effects on Achievement

Study 4A looked at long-term trend NAEP results in reading and mathematics for eighth and twelfth grades from 1971 to 2004: it found no effect of the introduction of high school exit exams for either lower or higher performing students (Grodsky et al., 2009, Tables 3-4). Over four combinations of subject and grade, the average effect size was 0.00 standard deviations, evenly divided between small positive and negative effects, and none was statistically significant.[16]

Examples 4B and 4C: Effects on Graduate Rates

Two studies looked at effects on graduation rates. Study 4B used state graduation rates from 1975 to 2002: it found that states adopting more difficult exit exams showed a statistically significant decrease in graduation rates of 2.1 percentage points (Warren et al., 2006, Table 2).[17] This result came from an analysis using Common Core Data that distinguished a high school diploma from a GED (general education development) certificate. An alternate analysis based on census data that used a graduation measure that combined high school diplomas and GED certificates showed no effect of exit exams: this result suggests that the requirement may shift some students from a obtaining a diploma to obtaining a GED.[18]

Study 4C used individual census data for 2000 with state fixed effects that identified changes resulting from exit exam requirements: it found that the requirements for more difficult exams were associated with a decrease in high school graduation—including both diplomas and GED certificates—of about 0.6 percentage points (Dee and Jacob, 2007, Table 6-2).[19] Over three different model specifications, all estimates were negative, and two of them were statistically significant. For the less difficult exit exams, Dee and Jacob (2007) found an average decrease of 0.3 percentage points, with only one of the three estimates statistically significant.

---

[16]We used the coefficients in the "HSEE" line of Table 3 of Grodsky et al. (2009, Table 2), dividing each by the standard deviation for reading and math scores, respectively.

[17]We used the estimates based on the Common Core Data with the model that distinguishes between minimum competency and more difficult exit exams (Warren et al., 2006, Table 2).

[18]Outcomes for high school graduates with a regular diploma are substantially better than those with a GED so it is better to distinguish the two outcomes (National Research Council and National Academy of Education, 2011).

[19]We averaged the three estimates in the "More difficult exit exam" line of Table 6-2 of Dee and Jacob (2007) for columns (3), (4), and (5).

The analyses looking at the effect of exit exams on graduation rates were not able to distinguish results for lower and higher performing students, though it is reasonable to expect that the requirements primarily affected lower performing students. Dee and Jacob (2007) also looked at college attendance, employment and earnings, and they found no overall effect from exit exam adoption.

EXPERIMENTS USING REWARDS

We identified causal studies related to 11 different experiments—in both the United States and in other countries—with rewards as the incentive for high performers. In the discussion below, we identify the experiments primarily grouped by location, in two cases clustering together several different but related experiments that were performed in the same location. The order of the discussion is alphabetical: India (one example), Israel (three examples), Kenya (two examples), Nashville (one example), New York City (one example), Ohio (one example), the Teacher Advancement Program in the United States (one example,), and Texas (one example).

Example 5: India

The Indian state of Andhra Pradesh conducted a 2-year experiment with teacher performance pay in rural elementary schools (Muralidharan and Sundararaman, 2011). The program randomly assigned schools to receive schoolwide incentives, individual teacher incentives, or to serve as a control group. The study also included two conditions that involved supplying extra resources in the form of either an additional teacher or cash for school materials. Each of the five conditions included 100 schools, with a typical school having three teachers and around 100 students. The performance pay in the two incentive conditions was based on average gains in student test scores in mathematics and language, measured either for the school as a whole in the schoolwide incentives condition or for the teacher's own students in the individual teacher incentives condition. The experiment used specially designed tests that explicitly included both basic and higher order skills,[20] and also included tests on science and social studies that did not receive incentives. The bonuses averaged about 3 percent of annual pay. The two incentive conditions did not include other types of support.

Averaged over the 2 years of the program, the test scores for the

---

[20]As a result of the use of both a broad test and an indicator based on gains (rather than a single proficiency level), this study was one of the few that has a "broad" performance measure within subjects (see Table 1).

schools in the two incentive conditions were 0.19 standard deviations higher than the control schools (Muralidharan and Sundararaman, 2011, Table 3).[21] The effects in both years were positive and statistically significant. Scores increased in both subjects, though the difference was larger for mathematics than language. Scores were higher in the two incentive conditions for both lower and higher performing students, with no statistically significant interaction of the incentive effect with student baseline score (Table 6 and Figure 3). The study did not include results on low-stakes tests in mathematics and language. However, scores on low-stakes tests in two subjects that were not a focus of the incentive program—science and social studies—were higher in the two incentive conditions, by an average of 0.14 standard deviations over 4 combinations of subject and year, with all 4 effects positive and statistically significant (Table 7). There was no difference between the effect of schoolwide and individual teacher incentives in the first year but the individual incentive schools performed statistically significantly higher in the second year. Over the 2 years, the average effect was 0.22 standard deviations for the individual incentives and 0.15 standard deviations for the schoolwide incentives (Table 8).[22]

The study included information about changes in teacher behavior that was obtained from direct observation and teacher interviews. Direct observation was conducted at each school several times during the 2 school years. There were no significant differences between the incentive and control schools in the direct observations measures of classroom process and teacher activity. In particular, the high level of teacher absenteeism—roughly 25 percent—was not affected by the incentives. In interviews, however, teachers in the incentive conditions reported higher levels of homework, classwork, instructional time, test preparation, and attention to lower performing students than did teachers in the control schools (Muralidharan and Sundararaman, 2009, Table 9). These reported differences were large and statistically significant in all cases, and in three cases were significantly correlated with student test scores.

The two resource conditions increased test scores by an average of 0.09 standard deviations over the 2 years of the program (Muralidharan

---

[21]We averaged the effects in the "Incentive School" row of Panel A for the columns that included school and household controls (Muralidharan and Sundararaman, 2011, Table 3). Our average included the results for the first and second year; the effects were 0.17 and 0.22 standard deviations, respectively.

[22]We averaged the effects in the "Individual Incentive School" and "Group Incentive School" rows, respectively, for column [1] for "Year 1 on Year 0" and for column [4] for "Year 2 on Year 0" in Table 8 of Muralidharan and Sundararaman (2011).

and Sundararaman, 2009, Table 10).[23] The effect of the resource conditions over the control was statistically significant in both years, but the improvement in the resource conditions was also significantly lower than the improvement in the incentive conditions. The spending in the resource conditions was chosen to roughly equal the spending in the incentive conditions, so the higher increases in the incentive conditions suggests that they might have been more cost effective. However, it is likely that the test scores in the incentive conditions were inflated by the attachment of the incentives while the test scores in the resource conditions were not; as a result, a valid comparison of the incentive and resource conditions cannot be made.

Examples 6, 7, and 8: Israel

Three different experiments in Israel were conducted to provide incentives to increase the number of students passing the *bagrut*, a high school certification typically earned by students who intend to go to college (Angrist and Lavy, 2009; Lavy 2002, 2009). (The *bagrut* is comparable to college-bound certificates in other countries such as the baccalaureate in France and the A-levels in the United Kingdom.) Unlike most of the other incentive programs that we discuss, the tests that formed the basis for the experiments in Israel were voluntary and also involved some choice about subjects and levels of difficulty. As a result, the programs could potentially have affected the number and difficulty of the tests taken, as well as the passing rate. Students must receive a total of 20 credits to earn the *bagrut* certificate, with each test worth 1 to 5 credits, depending on its difficulty.

The first program—Example 6—provided schoolwide incentives to teachers in comprehensive high schools, a school that includes grades 7-12 and covers two-thirds of the Israeli population (Lavy, 2002). The rewards were distributed to all teachers in winning schools in proportion to their salaries, with the resulting bonuses ranging from $250 to $1,000 at a time when the mean teacher salary was about $30,000. The program was designed as a tournament so that only schools in the top one-third received bonuses. Performance was based on three measures—credits earned per student, the proportion of students receiving the certificate, and the dropout rate—and was adjusted for the level of performance expected given the background of the students in the school. The 3-year program included 62 schools of the 170 comprehensive high schools in Israel. The typical school in the study had roughly 70-90 teachers and

---

[23]We averaged the results in the "Inputs" row for "Year 1 on Year 0" in column [1] and "Year 2 on Year 0" in column [4] in Table 10 of Muralidharan and Sundararaman (2011).

500-1,500 students (Lavy, 2002, Table 1). The incentives program did not provide additional forms of support.[24]

The second program—Example 7—provided individual incentives to teachers in grades 10-12 who were teaching classes in English, mathematics, or another core subject that would prepare students for one of the *bagrut* tests (Lavy, 2009). Rewards were based on the passing rate and the mean score for each class, with an adjustment that reflected expected performance based on student and school characteristics. Teachers received bonuses if their classes exceeded the expected results by a large amount, with bonuses per class ranging from $1,750 to $7,500. Since some teachers prepared multiple classes for exams, the bonuses could be large relative to the mean teacher salary of $30,000. The program was implemented at 49 comprehensive high schools that typically had low numbers of students who received the *bagrut*. The program included 629 teachers: 302 teachers received rewards, 16 of whom received rewards for two classes. The high schools included in the program had a combined senior class size of roughly 7,000 students. The program was expected to last 3 years but was discontinued after 1 year because of budget cuts. The program also did not provide additional forms of support.

The third program—Example 8—provided monetary incentives to students for passing *bagrut* tests (Angrist and Lavy, 2009). The program was implemented in 20 nonvocational high schools with low proportions of students who receive a *bagrut*. The incentives included small rewards for continuing in high school to the eleventh and twelfth grades and for taking any of the *bagrut* tests. Larger rewards were given for passing the tests, with the largest reward given for earning the 20 credits needed for a certificate. Students who received all the awards would have received an amount equal to roughly four months of full-time work at a typical wage for high school dropouts and students who work during the summer. However, as with the teacher incentives program (Example 8), the student incentives program was planned for 3 years but discontinued after only 1 year, so no students were able to receive awards in multiple years. The program included about 4,000 students (Angrist and Lavy, 2009, Table 1). Like Examples 6 and 7, the program did not provide additional forms of support.

For Examples 6 and 7, the high schools were selected in a way that made it possible to define a set of untreated schools to use as a control group in order to be able to draw causal conclusions. For the program with schoolwide teacher incentives (Example 6), the proportion of stu-

---

[24]Lavy (2002) contrasted the effect of the school incentives program with the results of a program implemented in 22 high schools in which extra teachers were used to help improve performance on the *bagrut* tests.

dents earning a certificate before the study was about 50 percent, and the program made no significant change in this overall proportion, though some specifications showed an increase of 3-4 percentage points, which approached significance (Lavy, 2002, Tables 1 and 2). Over 8 combinations of year, school type, and comparison group, the average increase was 2.2 percentage points.[25] None of the estimates of change in the certification rate was statistically significant; 6 were positive and 2 were negative. There were indications of increases in the proportion of students taking exams, the proportion achieving passing scores and the number of credits earned, though in the first year these increases appeared only for religious schools. Over 8 combinations of year, school type, and comparison group, the average effect of the incentives program on test scores was 0.11 standard deviations.[26] Six of the effect sizes were positive and statistically significant; two were not statistically significant, of which one was positive and one was negative. Information about contrasts in program effects for lower and higher performing students was not provided; however, using parents' schooling and family size as proxies for student performance, the analysis showed that the program effects were concentrated on lower performing students (Lavy, 2002, Table 3).

For the program that provided individual teacher incentives (Example 7), the analysis showed increases in both tests attempted and passed, as well as average scores (Lavy, 2009, Table 4). Over 2 subjects, math and English, the effect of the program on test scores averaged 0.19 standard deviations.[27] Using standard errors clustered by school and year, the effects were statistically significant for both subjects. Looking separately at students by quartile, there were positive and statistically significant effects on average test scores for the bottom three quartiles in math and the bottom quartile in English. For the top quartile in math and the top three quartiles in English, the effect on average test scores was small, mixed in sign, and not statistically significant (Table 4). The report on Example 7 did not provide information about changes in the proportion of students earning the *bagrut* certificate. A survey of teachers suggested that the incentives might have caused a number of changes in teaching methods and effort, including the use of individualized and small-group instruction, tracking students by ability, and the addition of instruction time, particularly before the tests (Table 8).

---

[25]We averaged the figures in columns [9] and [10] of Table 2 in Lavy (2002).

[26]We converted the score effects in columns [5] and [6] of Table 2 with the test score standard deviations of 21.088 and 19.780 for religious and secular schools, respectively, reported in Table 1 (Lavy, 2002).

[27]We converted the estimates in the "Treatment effect" row of the "Average score" section of Table 4 of Lavy (2009) into effect sizes by dividing by the average of the two test score standard deviations reported in the previous footnote from Lavy (2002). We used the estimates in columns (2) and (8) that cover all quartiles and use full controls.

For the program that provided student incentives (Example 8), the 20 high schools selected for the program were chosen randomly from a pool of 40 low-performing schools so that the schools not chosen for the program were an equivalent comparison group. The analysis focused on students who were seniors in the single year that the program operated, since these were the only students for whom the program operated as planned. The program produced a statistically significant increase in the proportion of girls earning a *bagrut* certificate of 10 percentage points; there was no effect for boys (Angrist and Lavy, 2009, Table 2, Panel A).[28]

When the effects for girls and boys were pooled together, the average increase in earning a certificate was 5.4 percentage points over 8 different model specifications, with all effects positive but none statistically significant (Table 2, Panel A, columns 1 and 2). The effect for girls was concentrated in the higher performing students; in these low-performing schools, only 50 percent of the higher performing girls received a certificate without the program and the incentives increased the proportion for these girls by about 20 percentage points (Table 4, Panel A, column 3). As with the other two programs, the student incentives increased both credits attempted and credits earned (Table 7, column 7). Surveys of students showed no effect of the program on study time, study effort, or paid employment, but the higher performing girls—the group for whom the program effect was concentrated—did show a statistically significant increase in participation in the marathon study sessions that are commonly held around the spring holidays (pp. 1,403-1,404).

Examples 6 and 8 point to a consistent finding that incentives can be used to increase the proportion of students earning a *bagrut* certificate, with the effect concentrated among students who are on the borderline of receiving a certificate. The effect was stronger in Example 8, using student incentives, which was targeted for high schools with low proportions of students earning a certificate: in that setting the affected students were in groups where 40-50 percent of the students earned a certificate. With the program with schoolwide incentives (Example 6), there was a weaker response, probably because the program included a wide range of schools: some were far below the 40-50 percent level where few students have a realistic chance of earning a certificate; and others were far above the 40-50 percent level, where most students would be expected to earn a certificate.[29] There was evidence that the incentive programs produced changes in the behavior of teachers and students, with more

---

[28] Angrist and Lavy (2009) referenced a number of studies on financial incentives in education that show stronger responses of females than males.

[29] In the program with schoolwide incentives, the standard deviation across schools in the proportion of students earning a certificate was about 50 percentage points (Lavy, 2002, Table 1).

focused instruction by teachers and increased effort by both teachers and students, primarily related to test preparation. The three programs did not include any low-stakes tests in the tested subjects to see whether the increased performance on the *bagrut* tests corresponded to more generalized achievement in those subjects.

Examples 9 and 10: Kenya

Two different experiments were conducted in primary schools in rural Kenya, one using schoolwide incentives to teachers and the other using incentives to students and their parents (Glewwe et al., 2010; Kremer et al., 2009). Both programs operated for 2 years. Primary schools in Kenya go through eighth grade, with a national test at the end that determines whether or not students go on to secondary school. Dropout rates in grades 5-7 are generally high in the country, with girls dropping out at a higher rate, and only one-third of all students finish the eighth grade (Kremer et al., 2009, p. 438).

The first incentives program—Example 9—provided schoolwide incentives to teachers on the basis of the students' average performance on district tests in grades 4-8 in seven subjects (Glewwe et al., 2010). Payments were given to schools that achieved either high scores or high score gains in a tournament across all the schools in the program. Although the performance indicator used gains, we coded the performance measure within subjects as "narrow" in Table 1 because the district tests relied solely on multiple choice questions (Glewwe et al., 2010, p. 211). The program included 50 schools, and 24 schools received prizes. In the winning schools, teachers of students in the tested grades received equal prizes, according to the school's rank in the tournament, with the prizes ranging from 21 to 43 percent of teachers' average monthly salary. The typical school had 12 teachers and 200 students, with roughly half in the grades affected by the program. No additional support was given as part of the program.

The second incentives program—Example 10—provided awards to students and their parents on the basis of students' performance on district tests in grade 6 in five subjects (Kremer et al., 2009). The program focused on girls, with the goal of increasing primary school completion among higher achieving girls. Prizes were given to the top 15 percent of girls according to their overall scores on the district exams. Winners were given money to pay for school fees and supplies for seventh and eighth grade. The program included 64 schools chosen randomly from a larger set (3 schools withdrew during the first year). Of the treated schools, 36 had at least one winner in the first year of the program, and 43 had at least one winner in the second year. No additional support was given as part of the program.

Examples 9 and 10 both randomly selected participating schools from a set of eligible schools so there was an experimental comparison group for analysis. In the program with schoolwide incentives to teachers (Example 9), test scores on the district exams were not significantly different during the first year; however, in the second year, the test scores increased by 0.14 standard deviations more than the comparison schools (Glewwe et al., 2010, Table 3, Panel A, columns 5 and 6). Over the 2 years, the average effect size on the high-stakes tests was 0.09 standard deviations. Low-stakes tests given by the organization sponsoring the experiment were mixed in sign and showed no significant effects, with an average effect of 0.01 standard deviations (Table 3, Panel B, columns 5 and 6). The district tests used in the program did not show any statistically significant increase in scores in program schools the year after the incentives ended, though the effect was positive (Table 3, Panel A, column 7).

Consistent with the incentives, which assigned a low score to students who did not take the exam, the first program increased the number of students taking the district tests by 7 percentage points averaged over the 2 years (Glewwe et al., 2010, Table 2, Panel B, columns 2 and 3). The program did not result in any significant changes in teacher attendance, homework assignment, or various measures of instruction (which were coded by trained observers) (Table 5, columns 4 and 5).[30]

In the program with incentives to students and their parents (Example 10), test scores on the district tests for girls increased by 0.12-0.19 standard deviations (Kremer et al., 2009, Table 4). The implementation of the program in one of the two districts was marred by low levels of trust with the sponsoring organization and a fatal lightning strike in a primary school; an analysis restricted to the Busia district, which did not experience these problems, showed an increase of 0.19-0.27 standard deviations in the district tests. Over 6 combinations of district, baseline control, and sample, the average effect size on the high-stakes tests was 0.20 standard deviations, with 4 of the effects statistically significant.[31] The test score effects occurred for both lower and higher performing girls within the

---

[30]As with the schools in the incentive programs in India, the teachers in the programs in Kenya had a high rate of absenteeism, averaging roughly 20 percent (Glewwe et al., 2010, p. 206).

[31]We averaged the program school estimates for the Busia and Teso districts combined and the Busia district separately, for analyses for the intention to treat (ITT), restricted, and longitudinal samples of Table 4 of Kremer et al. (2009). For the restricted sample estimates, we used the analysis with controls for mean school test scores in the year before the program began. For the longitudinal sample estimates, we used the analysis with controls for individual school test scores in the year before the program began.

schools (Kremer et al., 2009, p. 447). In Busia, the increased performance by the first cohort of girls on the district tests in the year of the program continued in their performance on the district tests the following year, when they were no longer in the program (0.24 standard deviations, p. 452), with the program affecting both girls who won prizes and girls who did not. The Busia girls in the first cohort also took a low-stakes test given by the sponsoring organization in the year after being in the program, and they showed an increased performance of 0.19 standard deviations above the girls who had been in control schools (p. 452). Both of these effects in the year following participation in the program by the first cohort Busia girls were statistically significant. A survey about attitudes related to education found no evidence that the incentives program affected student motivation (Table 8, Panel A).

There was some suggestion that the second program also improved outcomes for boys as well, even though they were not the focus of the program (Kremer et al., 2009, Table 5). There was no indication of significant program impacts on student attitudes, study habits, or available educational materials (Table 8). Unlike the school incentive programs in Kenya and the school and teacher incentive programs in India, the student and parent incentives program in Kenya increased teacher attendance by about 5 percentage points (Table 7).

Example 11: Nashville

A 3-year experiment conducted in the Metropolitan Nashville School System provided incentive pay to middle school mathematics teachers (Springer et al., 2010). A total of 296 teachers volunteered to participate in the experiment and were randomly assigned to treatment and control groups. Teachers in the treatment group were eligible to receive annual bonuses of $5,000-$15,000 on the basis of a value-added measure of change in the test scores of their students on the Tennessee state mathematics test. Although the performance indicator used changes in test scores rather than a single proficiency target, we coded the performance measure within subjects as "narrow" because the Tennessee state tests used only multiple-choice questions for mathematics.[32] The performance levels for receiving a bonus were set between the 85th and 95th percentiles of the districtwide distribution for the value-added measure. The proportion of participating teachers who received a bonus increased from one-third in the first year to one-half in the third year (Springer et al., 2010, Table 1). Over the course of the experiment, half of the teachers became ineligible to continue participating in the program, in most cases because they

---

[32]See Hightower (2010), state table for Standards, Assessments, and Accountability.

stopped teaching middle school mathematics in the district (Table 3). No additional support was provided as part of the incentives program.

Over 3 years and four grades, the average effect of the incentive program was 0.04 standard deviations on the high-stakes test, which was not statistically significant (Springer et al., 2010, p. 29). Over all 12 combinations of year and grade, the effects were positive in 7 of 12 cases, and 2 of them were statistically significant; of the 5 cases with negative effects, none of them was statistically significant (Table 7). For grades 5 and 6 the effects were all positive; for grades 7 and 8 all effects but one were negative. The effect for grade 5 was statistically significant in two of three cases. The students in grade 5 in the second year of the experiment, associated with one of the two significant effects in grade 5, did not perform significantly differently in mathematics the following year (p. 30). The study also looked at effects in reading, science, and social studies for the students of teachers in the experiment. There were no statistically significant effects for reading, but there were some statistically significant effects for science and social studies in grade 5, the same grade for which statistically significant effects appeared for mathematics (Springer et al., 2010, Tables C-1 to C-3).

Example 12: New York City

Fryer (2010) reports results of student incentive experiments carried out over 2 years in four urban school districts. In one of the districts—New York City—students were provided incentives on the basis of 10 interim tests in reading and mathematics that were designed to provide information related to the state standards and exams.[33] The fourth graders in the study could earn up to $25 on each test, and the seventh graders could earn up to $50 on each test, with the reward based on the score. The average fourth grader earned $139.43 and the average seventh grader earned $231.55 (Fryer, 2010, Table 1). Because the tests were designed to mirror the state exams, which include extended response items,[34] we coded the performance indicator as "broad." A total of 63 schools were randomly chosen to participate in the experiment out of 143 volunteer schools that included more than 17,000 students.

---

[33]In the other cities, the incentives were based on grades (Chicago), books read (Dallas), or attendance and behavior (Washington, DC). In Chicago, the effect of incentives based on grades was negative but small and not statistically significant (Fryer, 2010, Table 2). In Dallas, the effect of incentives based on books read was large and statistically significant for English speakers for measures of reading comprehension and language use but not vocabulary (Table 3). In Washington, DC, the effect of incentives based on attendance and behavior was moderate and positive but of marginal statistical significance (Table 3).

[34]See Hightower (2010), state table for Standards, Assessments, and Accountability.

The study reports the effect of the incentive program on the New York state tests in reading and mathematics.[35] Over eight combinations of subject, grade, and specification, the average effect size for the incentive programs was 0.01, with the effect sizes evenly distributed between positive and negative effects; none was statistically significant.[36] Considering the effects separately by subject, the average effect size was 0.00 for reading and 0.03 for mathematics, with each subject having two positive and two negative effects. Considering the effects separately by grade, the average effect size was 0.03 for fourth grade and 0.00 for seventh grade, with each grade having two positive and two negative effects. A separate assessment of student interest and enjoyment in schoolwork did not find a statistically significant change in motivation from the program, but the measured change was negative (Table 7).

Example 13: Ohio

A 3-year experiment in Coshocton, Ohio, a disadvantaged community, paid elementary school students in grades 3-6 for their scores on the state accountability tests in five core subjects (Bettinger, 2010). Students were paid $15 for each score at or above the 75th percentile and $20 for each score at or above the 85th percentile. All of the four elementary schools in Coshocton participated in the program at some time. The schools included roughly 900 students. No additional supports were provided by the program.

With four participating grades and four elementary schools, there were 16 grade-school combinations, half of which were randomly chosen each year to receive incentives under the program. The program resulted in a statistically significant increase of 0.13-0.19 standard deviations in the scores of the mathematics tests attached to the incentives (Bettinger, 2010, Table 3), but the effects on scores in reading, science, and social studies were small and not statistically significant, though all but one were positive (Tables 6 and 7). Information was not provided on the effect of the program on the writing test. Over 14 combinations of subject and model specification, the average effect on the high-stakes test was 0.06, with 4 of the 14 effects positive and statistically significant.[37] The effect in mathematics was concentrated on the lowest and highest quartile (Table 5).

---

[35] Given our criteria for coding the tests, we coded this as an example of a "low-stakes" test, since the state tests were not the tests that were being attached to the incentives in the experiment.

[36] We used the New York City estimates in Table 2 on the lines "Reading: All Controls" and "Math: All Controls" of Fryer (2010).

[37] We averaged the coefficients in the "Treatment" line of Tables 3, 6, and 7 of Bettinger (2010).

The study did not provide results for a low-stakes test. The study checked for spillover effects on siblings of students in classrooms with incentives: over four combinations of subject and model specifications, the effects on the siblings were consistently negative but none approached statistical significance (Table 10). Measures of changes in student motivation for academic tasks found no significant effects (p. 16).

Example 14: Teacher Advancement Program

The Teacher Advancement Program (TAP) is a comprehensive school reform model for the United States, developed by a foundation, that includes teacher performance pay (Glazerman et al., 2009; Glazerman and Seifullah, 2010; Springer et al., 2008). The performance award is based on value-added measures of the test score gains on the state achievement tests in both the teacher's individual class and averaged across the entire school, in addition to classroom observations by certified evaluators. Because the performance indicator includes both test score gains and classroom observations, we coded the performance measure within subjects as "broad." Rewards per teacher range up to $12,000, though the exact structure of the program varies by location (Springer et al., 2008).[38] As of 2007, the program had been implemented in more than 180 schools across the country, which includes roughly 5,000 teachers and 60,000 students. In addition to performance pay, TAP includes professional development and a system of multiple career paths to allow teachers to take on mentoring roles.

Example 14A: TAP in Chicago

Glazerman and colleagues studied the implementation of TAP in Chicago—Example 14A—using a hybrid experimental design in which treated schools were randomly assigned to year of implementation and were also matched to non-TAP control schools (Glazerman et al., 2009; Glazerman and Seifullah, 2010). Thus far, there are results for 2 years for the first cohort of schools and 1 year for the second cohort of schools. There were eight TAP elementary (K-8) schools in each cohort.[39] The studies analyzed changes in the test scores of the tests attached to the

---

[38]In the Chicago implementation of TAP, performance pay was phased in so that it was smaller during the first year of the program than it was in the second year. In the first cohort of schools, the first year bonus averaged $1,100, ranging from $0 to $2,045, and the second year bonus averaged $2,653, ranging from $0 to $6,320 (Glazerman and Seifullah, 2010, Table I.1).

[39]The TAP implementation in Chicago also included two high schools in each year, but the studies did not analyze their results because of the difficulty in finding appropriate controls.

incentives. The first-year study found effect sizes of −0.04 for both reading and mathematics, but neither effect was statistically significant. Across the 10 combinations of subject and grade in the study, 2 of the 10 effect sizes were positive and 8 were negative, and none was statistically significant (Glazerman et al., 2009, Tables IV.1 and IV.2). The second-year study found effect sizes of 0.00 for reading and 0.02 for mathematics, neither of which was statistically significant. Across the 10 combinations of subject and grade, 6 of the effect sizes were positive and 4 were negative, with none being statistically significant. (Glazerman and Seifullah, 2010, Tables III.1 and III.2).

The studies also looked at the effect of TAP on teacher retention.[40] In the first year, the first cohort showed a statistically significant increase in teacher retention at the school level of 5.2 percentage points (Glazerman et al., 2009, Table IV.5); this increase was concentrated in academic teachers who were not in the tested grades and subjects. In the second year, there was an increase in retention of 1.0 percentage point, which was not statistically significant (Glazerman and Seifullah, 2010, Table IV.1).

Example 14B: A Comparison of Mathematics Test Scores

Another study of TAP (Springer et al., 2008)—Example 14B— compared mathematics test score growth in schools that implemented TAP and schools that did not, using two different ways of controlling statistically for unobservable differences between the two types of schools. Over a 4-year period, the study analyzed data in two states for 1,200 schools in which 28 schools implemented TAP. To measure achievement growth, the study used fall-to-spring gains on the Northwest Evaluation Association (NWEA) tests in mathematics, given in grades 2-10, which were not attached to the incentives program. In grades 2-5, TAP schools increased test score gains by 1-2 points (Springer et al., 2008, Tables 6-7). The gains were statistically significant and correspond to an effect of roughly 0.2 standard deviations on gains that typically have a standard deviation of 7-8 points. In grades 6-8, the changes in TAP schools were small and mixed, with the only statistically significant changes being decreases of about 1 point for two grades in one of the two models. In grades 9-10, both models showed statistically significant decreases of 1-3 points. Over 18 combinations of grade and model specification, the aver-

---

[40]The focus of the analysis appears to be on retention resulting from the effects of voluntary turnover, not retention resulting from involuntary personnel decisions.

age effect was 0.01 standard deviations, with 13 of the 18 effects statistically significant, 7 of them positive and 6 of them negative.[41]

Example 15: Texas

A nonprofit organization in Texas started a program in 1996 that provides rewards to students and teachers for scores on advanced placement (AP) course exams (Jackson, 2010). As of 2007, the program included more than 40 secondary schools with high numbers of disadvantaged students. AP teachers receive payments of $500-$1,000 for each of their students who earns a score of 3 or higher on the AP test. Students receive a bonus of $100-$500 for each score of 3 or higher. Students must be enrolled in the corresponding AP course in order to earn the bonus from an AP test. The program also provides bonuses to teachers for being part of the program, ranging from $500-$1,000 for teachers in pre AP courses to $3,000-$10,000 for the lead teachers who organize and provide training for the AP program in a school. In addition to the financial rewards, the program includes teacher training, as well as a curriculum for the earlier grades to help prepare students for AP courses. Support for the program is provided primarily by private donors, who have some role in selecting a school and choosing which AP subjects will be rewarded and how large the rewards will be. The subjects typically included in the program are English, mathematics, and one or more of the sciences.

Jackson (2010) compared changes in outcomes in schools that adopted the AP incentive program to the changes in outcomes in schools that had chosen to adopt the program but had not yet done so because no donor had been found. The analysis measured student achievement with SAT and ACT test results, using a criterion of 1,100 on the SAT and 24 on the ACT. In schools selected for the program, 20 percent of graduates met the criterion on the SAT or ACT in the preferred model (Jackson, 2010, Table 2, model 28). In the schools that implemented the program, the proportion of graduates who met the criterion increased by 2 percentage points the first year and by 1 additional percentage point each in the second and in third years (Table 7, column 1). There was no significant change in the number of students who took the SAT or ACT (Table 2, model 22). There was no significant increase in AP course enrollment for the first 2 years

---

[41]We computed the average from the coefficients on the "TAP" line of Tables 6 and 7 in Springer et al. (2008) and then divided by a standard deviation of 7.5 because the NWEA tests in the elementary grades have a standard deviation of 7-8 points (p. 11). We did not have direct information about the standard deviation of the NWEA tests in the upper grades and so used 7.5 as the estimate for all grades. We did not use the results in Table 5, which did not control for selection of schools into the program and therefore did not support a causal interpretation about its effect.

of the program, but starting in the third year, enrollment increased by 34 percent (Table 3, column 1). There was an increase of 1.2 percent in the graduation rate, but the result was not statistically significant (Table 2, model 16). However, the number of students attending college increased by 5.3 percent (Table 2, model 34).

CONCLUSIONS

In this section we synthesize the results across the different incentive programs discussed above and summarized at the end of this chapter in Tables 4-1A, 4-1B, 4-2, and 4-3. We focus specifically on summarizing the types of incentive programs investigated and analyzing the effect of those programs on student achievement and on high school graduation and certification. We then consider the relative costs and benefits of incentive programs.

Types of Incentive Programs Investigated in the Literature

As summarized in Tables 4-1A and 4-1B, researchers and policy makers have explored incentive programs with a relatively wide range of variation in key structural features. Across the 15 examples we analyzed, there are substantial differences in who receives incentives, the breadth of the performance measures across and within subjects that are attached to the incentives, the nature of the consequences that the program attaches to the performance level, and whether extra support is provided by the program. In addition, there are differences in the nature and frequency of the consequences attached to the performance measures that are summarized in the text describing the programs, though not coded in the table.

The research literature we reviewed (see Chapters 2 and 3) suggests that these key structural features could be critical to the successful operation of an incentive program, so it is notable that the literature includes examples of different options for the different features. Looking at the feature options one at a time, the studies we review provide examples of major contrasts that could potentially be important, and for each contrasting feature option in the table, there are at least several strong studies that investigate programs containing that option.

When we considered the feature options in combination, however, it is clear that many possible combinations of the basic structural features do not appear: see Tables 4-1A and 4-1B. Some unexplored combinations are likely to seem uninteresting to implement as actual programs—such as a possible incentive program that might combine consequences in the form of sanctions while providing no additional support, which would likely prove to be politically untenable. However, there are a number of unexplored feature combinations that are potentially interesting and seem potentially promising for implementation and study.

In the current policy context, there are at least two such unexplored combinations of structural features that are salient: the combination of incentives for schools and broad performance measures within subjects, and the combination of incentives for individual teachers and sanctions.

The first combination is a frequently mentioned possible change that might be introduced with the next reauthorization of the Elementary and Secondary Education Act (ESEA)—school accountability with performance measures that have broader coverage within subjects by using tests that better reflect higher order thinking skills and indicators that are sensitive to changes across a broader range of performance than a single proficiency level.

The second combination is a frequently mentioned possible change in discussions about teacher quality—incentives for individual teachers in the form of sanctions that require teachers whose students do not meet some test-based level of performance to leave the profession (see, e.g., Lang, 2010; Staiger and Rockoff, 2010). Proposals to use the results of student tests as an input into teacher tenure decisions—which can be interpreted as subjecting teachers to a strong sanction if their students perform poorly—are an example of this combination. We do not take a position on either of these proposals here or on other unexplored combinations that may be proposed. Instead, we note the twin points that the existing research literature contains information about the effects of incentive programs that use these features in other combinations, but it does not contain information about the effects of programs with these particular combinations of features.

Effects on Student Achievement and High School Graduation and Certification

We summarize the effects of the incentive programs on student achievement and high school graduation and certification in Tables 4-2 and 4-3. We discuss these effects in terms of four groupings of programs: NCLB and its predecessors, high school exit exams, programs using rewards in other countries, and programs using rewards in the United States.

NCLB and Its Predecessors

The four studies that we analyzed all provided information about the achievement effects of test-based incentives targeted at schools that are in the NCLB mold.[42] The studies showed average incentive effects on the low-stakes tests ranging from 0.04 to 0.22 standard deviations. Across the studies there were a number of individual effect estimates that were positive and statistically significant, though there were also many that were not statistically significant and some that were negative.

At first blush, the evidence of incentives on student achievement from these studies appears substantial. However, there are two important caveats. First, the statistically significant effects were concentrated in fourth grade math; in contrast, the results for eighth grade math and for reading for both grades were often not statistically significant and sometimes negative.

Second, the highest two estimates—0.22 and 0.12 standard deviations—were problematic. Both estimates came from analyses that excluded results for eighth grade reading, giving an unbalanced overall picture of the effects of the incentives on achievement. In addition, the highest estimate of 0.22 standard deviations came from comparisons between public and private schools that may have been affected by movement away from Catholic schools that occurred during the early years of NCLB. Without these two problematic estimates, the effects estimated by the research range from 0.04 to only 0.08 standard deviations.

Given these two caveats, the evidence related to the effects on achievement of test-based incentives to schools appears to be modest, limited in both size and applicability. Our preferred estimate for these programs is 0.08 standard deviations, reflecting the national results for both the pre-NCLB period by Lee (2008) and the NCLB period by Dee and Jacob (2011). A program with an effect size of 0.08 standard deviations would raise the achievement of students currently at the 50th percentile to the 53rd percentile. This gain is small, both by itself and in comparisons across nations: the highest achieving countries on international tests often perform a full standard deviation above the United States, measured in terms of the distribution of performance within the United States (see, e.g., Gonzales et al., 2008, Figure 14 for TIMSS 2007 mathematics). To achieve an increase of the magnitude needed to match the high performing countries would mean that students currently at the 50th percentile in the United States would have to increase their scores to the current 84th percentile. For underachieving groups, far more improvement would be needed because of the large achievement gaps in the United States (Hill et al., 2008, Table 2). Although an effect size of 0.08 standard deviations is small in comparison with the improvements the nation hopes to achieve, it is comparable to the effect

---

[42]One of the research papers was a meta-analysis covering 14 studies, many of which would meet our inclusion criteria if we had considered them separately.

sizes found for other promising interventions that have been evaluated using standardized tests with relatively broad subject coverage (Hill et al., 2008, Table 4). The influential Tennessee STAR experiment with class-size reduction was notable for achieving effect sizes ranging from 0.15 to 0.25 standard deviations (Finn and Achilles, 1999), though the gains from class-size reduction have been much smaller when they were instituted on a statewide basis (e.g., Stecher et al. 2001).

High School Exit Exams

One of the three studies on the effects of high school exit exam requirements provided estimates of the effects on achievement on a low-stakes test: it found an average effect of 0.00 standard deviations (see Table 4-2). The other two studies provided estimates of the effects on graduation: they found average effects of −2.1 and −0.6 percentage points (see Table 4-3). A number of the negative effects are statistically significant. The smaller estimate was for a study that counted GEDs as equivalent to high school diplomas; excluding this study leaves an estimate of the graduation effect of −2.1 percentage points.

Incentive Programs That Use Rewards in Other Countries

The committee's analysis included six studies of incentive programs that used rewards in other countries, in India, Israel, and Kenya. The Kenya study measured the effect of incentives on achievement using low-stakes tests, while the studies in India and Israel measured the achievement effect using the tests attached to the incentives (see Table 4-2). The six studies found average estimates of the effect on achievement ranging from 0.01 to 0.19 standard deviations, and most of the high positive effects are statistically significant. Two of the Israel studies found effects on high school certification that averaged 2.2 and 5.4 percentage points (see Table 4-3). The Israel studies found that the effects on both achievement and certification were concentrated on lower-performing students.

As with the studies on NCLB and its predecessors, the studies on foreign reward programs suggest substantial benefits of incentive programs that must be considered in light of important caveats. First, the programs in India and Israel measured achievement using the high-stakes tests attached to the incentives. The problems with this measure are discussed above, and it is not clear how much change in achievement would be shown on low-stakes tests.

Second, the programs in India and Kenya were in developing countries that have quite a different context for education than that in developed countries. In particular, the high level of teacher absenteeism and the high rate of student dropout in middle school suggest that the incentives for both teachers and students may operate differently in developing countries.

Given these caveats, it is not clear what can be learned from these studies that would be applicable to the use of incentives in the United States. For all three countries, there are difficulties in drawing conclusions about the ability of such programs to increase achievement in the United States. In addition, although the ability of the Israel programs to increase high school certification with incentives is potentially promising, it is hard to evaluate the value of the increase without knowing whether it is accompanied by increased learning beyond that measured by the high-stakes test.

U.S. Incentive Programs That Use Rewards

Six of the seven studies that provided information about U.S. incentive programs that use rewards showed average effects on achievement that ranged from −0.02 to 0.06 standard deviations (see Table 4-2). Many effects were positive, and some were statistically significant, but there were also a number of negative effects. The estimates of achievement effects included a number that were based on the tests attached to the incentives; when these are eliminated, there are two studies, both of which found 0.01 standard deviations. One study showed an effect of incentives on high school graduation of 0.9 percentage points, but the effect was not statistically significant (see Table 4-3).

On the basis of our synthesis of the evidence, summarized above, we reached two conclusions about the effect of test-based incentives on student achievement and high school completion.

Conclusion 1: Test-based incentive programs, as designed and implemented in the programs that have been carefully studied, have not increased student achievement enough to bring the United States close to the levels of the highest achieving countries. When evaluated using relevant low-stakes tests, which are less likely to be inflated by the incentives themselves, the overall effects on achievement tend to be small and are effectively zero for a number of programs. Even when evaluated using the tests attached to the incentives, a number of programs show only small effects. Programs in foreign countries that show larger effects are not clearly applicable in the U.S. context. School-level incentives like those of the No Child Left Behind Act produce some of the larger estimates of achievement effects, with effect sizes around 0.08 standard deviations, but the mea-

sured effects to date tend to be concentrated in elementary grade mathematics and the effects are small compared to the improvements the nation hopes to achieve.

Conclusion 2: The evidence we have reviewed suggests that high school exit exam programs, as currently implemented in the United States, decrease the rate of high school graduation without increasing achievement. The best available estimate suggests a decrease of 2 percentage points when averaged over the population. In contrast, several experiments with providing incentives for graduation in the form of rewards, while keeping graduation standards constant, suggest that such incentives might be used to increase high school completion.

Balancing the Benefits and Costs of Test-Based Incentives

The research to date suggests that the benefits of test-based incentive programs over the past two decades have been quite small. Although the available evidence is limited, it is not insignificant. The incentive programs that have been tried have involved a number of different incentive designs and substantial numbers of schools, teachers, and students. We focused on studies that allowed us to draw conclusions about the causal effects of incentive programs and found a significant body of evidence that was carefully constructed. Unfortunately, the guidance offered by this body of evidence is not encouraging about the ability of incentive programs to reliably produce meaningful increases in student achievement—except in mathematics for elementary school students.

Although the evidence to date about the effectiveness of incentive programs has not been encouraging, the basic research findings suggest a number of features that are likely to be important to the effectiveness of incentive programs and that can provide guidance in the design of new models. Some proposals for new models of incentive programs involve combinations of features that have not yet been tried to a significant degree, such as school-based incentives using broader performance measures and teacher incentives using sanctions related to tenure. Other proposals involve more sophisticated versions of the basic features we have described, such as the "trigger" systems discussed in Chapter 3 that use the more narrow information from tests to start an intensive school evaluation that considers a much broader range of information and then provides more focused supports to aid in school improvement.

It is also likely to be important to consider potential programs that focus more on the informational role that tests can play. Our study has specifically *not* focused on policies and programs that rely solely on information about educational achievement that tests provide to drive improvement through educator motivation and public pressure. Our focus for the study was chosen because so much of the educational policy discussion over the past decade has been driven by the conclusion that mere information without explicit consequences is insufficient to drive change. And yet the guidance coming from the basic research in psychology suggests that the purely informational uses of test results may be more effective in some situations than incentives that attach explicit consequences to those results. As policy makers and educators continue to look for successful routes to improving education in the years ahead, the exploration should include more subtle incentives that rely on the informational role of test results and broader types of accountability.

In continuing to explore promising routes to using test-based incentives, however, policy makers and educators should take into account the costs of doing so. Over the past two decades, the education policy and research communities have invested substantial attention and resources in exploring the use of test-based incentives as a way to improve education. This investment seemed to be worthwhile because it appeared to offer a promising route for improvement. Further investment in test-based incentives still seems to be worthwhile because there are now more sophisticated proposals for using test-based incentives that offer hope for improvement and deserve to be tried. However, in choosing how much attention and investment to devote to the exploration of new forms of test-based incentives, it is important to remember that there are other aspects of improving education that also would benefit from development. In addition to test-based incentives, investments to improve standards, curriculum, instructional methods, and educator capacity are all likely to be necessary for improving educational outcomes. Although these other aspects of the system are likely to be complements to test-based incentives in improving education, they are competitors for funding and policy attention. Further research and development of promising new approaches to test-based incentives need to be balanced against the research and development needs of promising new approaches in other areas related to improving education. We have not considered those trade-offs in our examination of test-based incentives, but those trade-offs are the most important costs that need to be considered by the policy makers who will decide which new incentive programs to support.

TABLE 4-1A Overview of Results from All Studies of Test-Based Incentive Programs Using Causal Analyses

	Structure of Incentives System[a]				
Incentive Programs	Target Who Receives Incentives	Perf Measure Across Subjects	Perf Measure Within Subjects	Conse-quences	Support
Studies of NCLB and Its Predecessors					
1. U.S. pre-NCLB	Schools	Mixed	Mixed	Mixed	Mixed
2A. U.S. NCLB	Schools	Narrow	Narrow	Sanction	Yes
2B. U.S. NCLB	Schools	Narrow	Narrow	Sanction	Yes
2C. U.S. NCLB	Schools	Narrow	Narrow	Sanction	Yes
3. Chicago pre-NCLB	Schools and Students	Narrow	Narrow	Sanction	Yes
Studies of High School Exit Exams					
4. U.S. HS Exit	Students	Mixed	Narrow	Sanction	Yes
Studies of Incentive Experiments Using Rewards					
5. India	Teachers-I or Teachers-G	Narrow	Broad	Reward	No
6. Israel Teachers-G	Teachers-G	Broad	Narrow	Reward	No
7. Israel Teachers-I	Teachers-I	Broad	Narrow	Reward	No
8. Israel Student	Students	Broad	Narrow	Reward	No
9. Kenya Teachers-G	Teachers-G	Broad	Narrow	Reward	No
10. Kenya Student	Students and Parents	Broad	Narrow	Reward	No
11. Nashville	Teachers-I	Narrow	Narrow	Reward	No
12. New York	Students	Narrow	Broad	Reward	No
13. Ohio Student	Students	Broad	Narrow	Reward	No
14A. TAP-Chicago	Teachers-I and Teachers-G	Broad	Broad	Reward	Yes
14B. TAP-2 states	Teachers-I and Teachers-G	Broad	Broad	Reward	Yes
15. Texas AP	Teachers-I and Students	Narrow	Narrow	Reward	Yes

NOTE: Teachers-G = Teachers-Group, Teachers-I = Teachers-Individually.

[a]The features related to the structure of incentive programs that should be considered when designing the programs are (1) the target for the incentives (schools, teachers, or students in these examples); (2) the extent to which the performance measures are aligned with the outcomes desired (broad or narrow), both across and within subjects; (3) the consequences that the incentives provide (reward or sanction); (4) the support provided to reach the performance goals; and (5) the way the incentives are framed and communicated. The last feature is not included in the table because no studies consider it.

TABLE 4-1B Overview of Results from All Studies of Test-Based Incentive Programs Using Causal Analyses

Incentive Programs	Outcomes[a]					
	Effect on High-Stakes Tests	Effect on Low-Stakes Tests	Effect on Other Subject Tests	Effect on HS Grad or Cert	Effect on Lower Perf Students	Effect on Higher Perf Students
Studies of NCLB and Its Predecessors						
1. U.S. pre-NCLB		+				
2A. U.S. NCLB		0/+	0		+/0	+/0
2B. U.S. NCLB		0/+				
2C. U.S. NCLB		0/+				
3. Chicago pre-NCLB	+	0/+/−	+		+	+/0
Studies of High School Exit Exams						
4. U.S. HS Exit		0		−/0	test 0	test 0
Studies of Incentive Experiments Using Rewards						
5. India	+		+		+	+
6. Israel Teachers-G	+			+/0	+	0
7. Israel Teachers-I	+				+	0
8. Israel Student				+	+	0
9. Kenya Teachers-G	+/0	0				
10. Kenya Student	+	+			+	+
11. Nashville	0/+		0/+			
12. New York	0					
13. Ohio Student	+/0				+/0	+/0
14A. TAP-Chicago	0					
14B. TAP-2 states		+/−/0				
15. Texas AP		+		0		+

NOTE: Teachers-G = Teachers-Group, Teachers-I = Teachers-Individually.

[a]Results of studies are characterized here as positive (+), negative (−), or not statistically significantly different from zero (0). The most lenient level of significance provided in the study is used, generally $p < 0.10$ or $p < 0.05$.

TABLE 4-2 Summary of Average Effects of Incentive Programs on Student Achievement Tests

| Incentive Programs | Test Outcome | | Distribution of Test Outcome Effects Across Analyses | | | |
	Type of Stakes	Overall Effect Size[a]	+Sig	+Nonsig	−Nonsig	−Sig
Studies of NCLB and Its Predecessors						
1. U.S. pre-NCLB	Low	0.08		87%		11%
2A. U.S. NCLB	Low	0.08	25%	50%	25%	0%
2B. U.S. NCLB	Low	0.12[b]	33%	67%	0%	0%
2C. U.S. NCLB	Low	0.22[c]	17%	83%	0%	0%
3. Chicago pre-NCLB	Low	0.04	83%	22%	22%	22%
Studies of High School Exit Exams						
4A. U.S. HS Exit	Low	0.00	0%	50%	50%	0%
Studies of Incentive Experiments Using Rewards						
5. India	High	0.19	100%	0%	0%	0%
6. Israel Teachers-G	High	0.11	75%	13%	13%	0%
7. Israel Teachers-I	High	0.19	100%	0%	0%	0%
9. Kenya Teachers-G	Low	0.01	0%	50%	50%	0%
10. Kenya Student	Low	0.19	100%	0%	0%	0%
11. Nashville	High	0.04	17%	42%	42%	0%
12. New York	Low	0.01	0%	50%	50%	0%
13. Ohio Student	High	0.06	29%	64%	7%	0%
14A. TAP-Chicago	High	−0.02	0%	50%	50%	0%
14B. TAP-2 states	Low	0.01	39%	11%	17%	33%

NOTE: Teachers-G = Teachers-Group, Teachers-I = Teachers-Individually.

[a]Effect size is presented in standard deviation units.

[b]Omits eighth grade reading.

[c]Omits eighth grade reading; uses comparison to private schools during period of fluctuating enrollment.

TABLE 4-3 Average Effects of Test-Based Incentive Programs on High School Graduation/Certification Rates

Incentive Programs	HS Grad/ Cert Rate Changes	Distribution of Rate Changes Across Analyses			
		+Sig	+Nonsig	−Nonsig	−Sig
Studies of High School Exit Exams					
4B. U.S. HS Exit	−2.1%	0%	0%	0%	100%
4C. U.S. HS Exit	−0.6%	0%	0%	33%	67%
Studies of Incentive Experiments Using Rewards					
6. Israel Teachers-G	2.2%	0%	75%	25%	0%
8. Israel Student	5.4%	0%	100%	0%	0%
15. Texas AP	0.9%	0%	50%	50%	0%

NOTE: Teachers-G = Teachers-Group.

5

Recommendations for Policy and Research

The preceding chapters have synthesized our key findings and conclusions from the basic research about the way that incentives operate and from the applied research about the results of implementing
test-based incentive policies in education. In this chapter, the committee
recommends ways to improve current test-based incentive policies and
highlights important directions for further research. We discuss the use
of test-based incentives, the design of test-based incentive programs, and
the research that is needed about those programs.

THE USE OF TEST-BASED INCENTIVES

As discussed in Chapter 4, there have been a number of careful efforts
to use test-based incentives to improve education. They have included
broadly implemented government policies—notably, state high school exit
exams and the school-level requirements of NCLB and its predecessors—as
well as experimental programs. A number of these programs have been
carefully studied, using research designs that allow some level of causal
conclusions about their effects. We conclude (see Chapter 4) that the available evidence does not give strong support for the use of test-based incentives to improve education and provides only minimal guidance about
which incentive designs may be effective. However, basic research related
to the design of incentives and the practical experience from implementing the first generation of incentive programs suggest more sophisticated
approaches to designing incentive programs that are promising and should

be investigated. As a result, we recommend that policy makers continue to support the development of new approaches to test-based incentives but with a realistic understanding of the limited knowledge about how to design such programs so that they will be effective.

> **Recommendation 1: Despite using them for several decades, policy makers and educators do not yet know how to use test-based incentives to consistently generate positive effects on achievement and to improve education.** Policy makers should support the development and evaluation of promising new models that use test-based incentives in more sophisticated ways as one aspect of a richer accountability and improvement process. However, the modest success of incentive programs to date means that all use of test-based incentives should be carefully studied to help determine which forms of incentives are successful in education and which are not. Continued experimentation with test-based incentives should not displace investment in the development of other aspects of the education system that are important complements to the incentives themselves and likely to be necessary for incentives to be effective in improving education.

It is only by continuing to conduct careful research about test-based incentive programs that it will be possible to understand how they can be more effectively designed. The small or nonexistent benefits that have been demonstrated to date suggest that incentives need to be carefully designed and combined with other elements of the educational system to be effective. Much additional work will be required to learn whether and how test-based incentives can be used to produce consistent improvements in education. The available evidence does not justify a single-minded focus on test-based incentives as a primary tool of education policy without a complementary focus on other aspects of the system.

THE DESIGN OF NEW PROGRAMS

The general lack of guidance coming from existing studies of test-based incentive programs in education suggests that future policy experimentation with test-based incentives should be guided by the key contrasts that emerge from basic research about how incentives operate.

> **Recommendation 2: Policy makers and researchers should design and evaluate new test-based incentive programs in ways that provide information about alternative approaches to incen-**

tives and accountability. This should include exploration of the effects of key features suggested by basic research, such as who is targeted for incentives; what performance measures are used; what consequences are attached to the performance measures and how frequently they are used; what additional support and options are provided to schools, teachers, and students in their efforts to improve; and how incentives are framed and communicated. Choices among the options for some or all of these features are likely to be critical in determining which—if any—incentive programs are successful.

In general, the design of test-based incentives should begin with a clear description and delineation of the most valued educational goals that the incentive program is meant to promote, as well as recognition of the tradeoffs among these goals. Those goals should shape the features of the incentive program, even though experience shows that the effects of a program may not always occur in the ways intended.

The performance measures used in an incentive system are likely to be critical. The tests and indicators used for performance measures should be designed to reflect the most valued educational goals, and their relative weights in the incentive system should reflect the tradeoffs across educational goals that designers of the system are prepared to accept. Although any test will necessarily be incomplete, it should be designed to emphasize the most important learning goals in the subject domain and to measure students' attainment of the goals through the use of various test item formats.

A test that asks very similar questions from year to year and uses a limited set of item formats will become predictable and encourage narrow teaching to the test. The test scores are likely to become distorted as a result, even if they were initially an excellent measure. To reduce the inclination for teachers to inappropriately teach to high-stakes tests, the tests themselves should be designed to sample the subject domain broadly and include continually changing content and item formats. And test items should be reused only rarely and unpredictably.

Performance targets should be challenging while also being attainable. Data should be used to determine attainable targets. Psychological research shows that unrealistically high goals undermine motivation. The ideal goals provide optimal challenge—ones that encourage people to stretch themselves and are attainable with effort.

The indicators used to summarize test results should match the goals of the test-based incentives policy, both in terms of the level of student achievement expected and the students or subgroups that are the focus of attention. Because any system of tests and indicators is necessarily incomplete, the system should be designed to emphasize the most important goals, and progress toward those goals should be measured in varied and diverse ways. Policy makers should recognize that goals that are not measured are likely to be deemphasized during instruction. Test-based incentive systems should be dynamic, responding to current goals as well as to indications of whether incentives are aligned to these goals in practice.

Given that tests are necessarily incomplete measures of valued educational goals, designers of incentive systems should recognize the potential problems inherent in having strong consequences based on test scores alone and should experiment with the use of systems of multiple measures that reflect desired outcomes. One way of incorporating multiple measures would be to use the results of large-scale tests as triggers for more focused evaluation of struggling schools and teachers, rather than as final evaluations on their own.

It is possible that the weak effects of the test-based incentive programs we reviewed may be due in part to the use of performance measures based primarily on tests that encourage narrow test preparation rather than broader instruction that can produce more general learning gains that are not tied to a particular test. We note, however, that the one program we reviewed that used multiple measures—the Teacher Advancement Program, which uses classroom observations in addition to test scores in evaluating teachers—produced a near-zero average effect with a number of negative effects in the upper grades. Again, this result underlines how much is still unknown about using test-based incentives effectively.

The nature of the support provided in conjunction with a test-based incentives system is also likely to prove important to success. If the capacity to bring about change is limited, successful implementation will require that the incentives system include provisions to promote the development of that capacity. In any system of incentives—whether focused on schools, teachers, or students—the people who are most in need of improvement and therefore usually the focus of the incentives are often specifically those who lack the capacity to bring about change on their own. The research to date does not suggest what kinds of support could be paired with test-based incentives to increase program effectiveness.

It is beyond the committee's charge to suggest how to build capacity in school systems, but there is a growing literature on resources that are most useful in helping schools improve. Some of that work is brought together in two reports from the National Research Council, *Engaging Schools: Fostering High School Students' Motivation to Learn* (National Research Council and Institute of Medicine, 2004) and *America's Lab Report: Investigations in High School Science* (2006a). A recent report by the Center on Reinventing Public Education (Hill et al., 2008) suggests new approaches to finance, governance, and accountability that would foster the kinds of competitive experimentation that could produce empirically grounded understandings of what works under what circumstances and for different groups.

RESEARCH ON TEST-BASED INCENTIVES

Substantial research needs to be conducted in order to understand the effects of test-based incentives well enough for policies to be designed that will consistently result in meaningful educational improvement. The committee recognizes that it is difficult and time-consuming to conduct definitive—or even credible—studies of the effects of test-based incentives in educational settings. However, there is a strong initial body of work that can serve as a foundation. Chapter 4 provides examples of the kind of research that will be needed to identify successful ways of designing test-based incentive policies.

> **Recommendation 3: Research about the effects of incentive programs should fully document the structure of each program and should evaluate a broad range of outcomes. To avoid having their results determined by the score inflation that occurs in the high-stakes tests attached to the incentives, researchers should use low-stakes tests that do not mimic the high-stakes tests to evaluate how test-based incentives affect achievement. Other outcomes, such as later performance in education or work and dispositions related to education, are also important to study. To help explain why test-based incentives sometimes produce negative effects on achievement, researchers should collect data on changes in educational practice by the people who are affected by the incentives.**

The committee offers priorities for rigorous research, presented as questions, in four areas: behavioral responses to incentives, validity of test score gains, incentive system outcomes, and incentive system improvements.

Behavioral Responses to Incentives

- What types of incentives do different types of performance measures and indicators create for educators and students?
- What is the range of effects—not just the average—of different types of incentives on teachers' and students' behavior and motivation?

- How does the complexity of an incentives system affect the ability of educators, parents, and students to understand the intended signals and respond to them?

Validity of Test Score Gains

- What is the relationship between the responses of teachers and others in the school system to test-based incentives and the validity of the gains in test scores? What measures of responses to accountability should be used to understand these relationships?
- What is the relationship between test-based incentives and external criteria, such as employment and wages? Are there relative wage and employment increases among the people for whom test scores rose?
- What characteristics of students, schools, and test-based incentives predict score inflation?
- What are some practical auditing methods, that is, cost-effective ways to monitor test score gains overall and at the school level?

Incentives System Outcomes

- What are the effects of test-based incentives on school and classroom practices? What changes occur in school policies, curriculum, instruction, and nonacademic activities, and are they consistent with community goals and priorities?
- What are the verifiable effects on student learning that can be attributed to the expectation of being accountable or to the subsequent use of data?
- How do test-based incentives affect the labor market for teachers, including recruitment, hiring, retention, placement, and mobility?
- How do stakeholders—students, parents, educators, policy makers, elected officials—affect the design and effects of test-based incentives?

Incentives System Improvements

- How can subjective measures of teaching practices be used to improve test-based incentives?
- How can large-scale tests be used as triggers to identify schools that need more focused, in-depth evaluation?
- What role should value-added analyses play in developing indicators for test-based incentives? What are the points of leverage in the education system for improvement? What are the policy and administrative levers for effecting change?

CLOSING REFLECTIONS

The charge to the committee pointed out the contradiction between many economists' optimism and most psychologists' pessimism about the potential for test-based incentives to alter academic performance. Our review of the literature and our deliberations did not resolve the contradiction. Our review of the evidence uncovered reasons to expect positive results from incentive programs and reasons to be skeptical of apparent gains. Our recommendations, accordingly, call for policy makers to support experimentation with rigorous evaluation and to allow midcourse correction of policies when evaluation suggests such correction is needed.

Our call for more research may seem like a hackneyed response, but we believe it is essential with regard to incentives. In calling for more evaluation, we draw attention to the fact that the frequent question, "Do incentives work?" is too broad and vague to be answerable. Most reforms using test-based incentives attempt to change student performance in many grades and many subjects. When ambitions are so broad, it is not surprising that the results are varied and unclear. Broad and major reforms do not succeed or fail all at once and altogether. Outcomes usually mix small successes and failures that add up to either modest improvements or disappointments. Our call for more focused evaluations is a call to examine the expected successes and failures. We call on researchers, policy makers, and educators to examine the evidence in detail and not to reduce it to a simple thumbs-up or thumbs-down verdict. The school reform effort will move forward to the extent that everyone, from policy makers to parents, learns from a thorough and balanced analysis of each success and each failure.

References

Abramson, L.Y., Seligman, M.E.P., and Teasdale, J.D. (1978). Learned helplessness in humans: Critique and reformulation. *Journal of Abnormal Psychology, 87*, 49-74.

American Educational Research Association, American Psychological Association, and National Council on Measurement in Education. (1999). *Standards for Educational and Psychological Testing*. Washington, DC: Author.

Angrist, J., and Lavy, V. (2009).The effects of high-stakes high school achievement awards: Evidence from a group-randomized trial. *American Economic Review, 99*(4), 1,384-1,414.

Archer, J. (2006). British inspectors bring instructional focus to NYC. *Education Week, 25*(37), 10.

Ariely, D. (2008). *Predictably Irrational: The Hidden Forces That Shape Our Decisions*. New York: HarperCollins.

Atkinson, J.W. (1964). *An Introduction to Motivation*. Princeton, NJ: Von Nostrand.

Baker, E.L., and Linn, R.L. (2004). Validity issues for accountability systems. In S.H. Fuhrman and R.F. Elmore (Eds.), *Redesigning Accountability Systems for Education*. New York: Teachers College Press.

Baker, G. (2002). Distortion and risk in optimal incentive contracts. *Journal of Human Resources, 37*, 728-751.

Benware, C., and Deci, E.L. (1984). Quality of learning with an active versus passive motivational set. *American Educational Research Journal, 21*, 755-765.

Bettinger, E.P. (2010). *Paying to Learn: The Effect of Financial Incentives on Elementary School Test Scores*. Working Paper 16333. Cambridge, MA: National Bureau of Economic Research.

Betts, J.R., and Costrell, R.M. (2001). Incentives and equity under standards-based reform. In D. Ravitch (Ed.), *Brookings Papers on Education Policy 2001*. Washington, DC: Brookings Institution Press.

Bishop, J.H., Mane, F., Bishop, M., and Moriarty, J. (2001). The role of end-of-course exams and minimum competency tests in standards-based reforms. In D. Ravitch (Ed.), *Brookings Papers on Education Policy* (pp. 267-346). Washington, DC: The Brookings Institution. Available: http://muse.jhu.edu/login?uri=/journals/brookings_papers_on_education_policy/v2001/2001.1bishop.pdf [September 2011].

Booher-Jennings, J. (2005). Below the bubble: "Educational triage" and the Texas accountability system. *American Educational Research Journal, 42*(2), 231-268.

Boyd, D.J., Grossman, P.L., Lankford, H., Loeb, S., and Wyckoff, J.H. (2009). *Who Leaves? Teacher Attrition and Student Achievement*. CALDER Working Paper 23. Washington, DC: Urban Institute Press.

Braun, H.I. (2005). *Using Student Progress to Evaluate Teachers: A Primer on Value-Added Models*. Princeton, NJ: Educational Testing Service.

Buckendahl, C.W., Smith, R., Impara, J.C., and Plake, B.S. (2002). A comparison of Angoff and bookmark standard setting methods. *Journal of Educational Measurement, 39*(3), 253-263.

Burawoy, M. (1979). *Manufacturing Consent: Changes in the Labor Process Under Monopoly Capitalism*. Chicago: University of Chicago Press.

Burgess, S., and Ratto, M. (2003). The role of incentives in the public sector: Issues and evidence. *Oxford Review of Economic Policy, 19*, 285-300.

California Department of Education. (2011) *Overview of California's 2010-2011 Accountability Progress Reporting System*. Sacramento: Author.

Cameron, J., and Pierce, W.D. (1994). Reinforcement, reward, and intrinsic motivation: A meta-analysis. *Review of Educational Research, 64*, 363-423.

Campbell, D.T. (1975). Assessing the impact of planned social change. In G. Lyons (Ed.), *Social Research and Public Policies: The Dartmouth/OECD Conference*. Hanover, NH: Dartmouth College Public Affairs Center.

Center on Education Policy. (2003). *From the Capital to the Classroom: State and Federal Efforts to Implement the No Child Left Behind Act*. Washington, DC: Author.

Center on Education Policy. (2005). *High School Exit Exams: States Try Harder, But Gaps Persist*. Washington DC: Author.

Center on Education Policy. (2006a). *From the Capital to the Classroom: Year 4 of the No Child Left Behind Act*. Washington, DC: Author.

Center on Education Policy. (2006b). *State High School Exit Exams: A Challenging Year*. Washington DC: Author.

Center on Education Policy. (2007a). *Choices, Changes, and Challenges: Curriculum and Instruction in the NCLB Era*. Washington, DC: Author.

Center on Education Policy. (2007b). *State High School Exit Exams: Working to Raise Test Scores*. Washington, DC: Author.

Center on Education Policy. (2008). *Has Student Achievement Increased Since 2002? State Test Score Trends Through 2006-2007*. Washington, DC: Author.

Center on Education Policy. (2010). *How Many Schools and Districts Have Not Made Adequate Yearly Progress? Four-Year Trends*. Washington, DC: Author.

Chester, M. (2005). Making valid and consistent inferences about school effectiveness from multiple measures. *Educational Measurement: Issues and Practice, 24*(4), 40-52.

Cronin, J., Kingsbury, G.G., McCall, M.S., and Bowe, B. (2005). *The Impact of the No Child Left Behind Act on Student Achievement and Growth: 2005 Edition*. Northwest Evaluation Association Technical Report. Lake Oswego, OR: Northwest Evaluation Association.

Csikszentmihalyi, M. (1990). *Flow*. New York: Harper and Row.

Cullen, J.B., and Reback, R. (2006). Tinkering toward accolades: School gaming under a performance accountability system. In T.J. Gronberg and D.W. Jansen (Eds.), *Improving School Accountability: Advances in Applied Microeconomics, Volume 14*. Bingley, UK: Emerald Group.

Deci, E.L. (1971). Effects of externally mediated rewards on intrinsic motivation. *Journal of Personality and Social Psychology, 18*, 105-115.

Deci, E.L. (1992). The relation of interest to the motivation of behavior: A self-determination theory perspective. In K.A. Renninger, S. Hidi, and A. Krapp, (Eds.), *The Role of Interest in Learning and Development* (pp. 43-70). Hillsdale, NJ: Lawrence Erlbaum Associates.

Deci, E.L., and Ryan, R.M. (1985). *Intrinsic Motivation and Self-Determination in Human Behavior.* New York: Plenum.

Deci, E.L., Schwartz, A.J., Sheinman, L., and Ryan, R.M. (1981). An instrument to assess adults' orientations toward control versus autonomy with children: Reflections on intrinsic motivation and perceived competence. *Journal of Educational Psychology, 73,* 642-650.

Deci, E.L., Spiegel, N.H., Ryan, R.M., Koestner, R., and Kauffman, M. (1982). Effects of performance standards on teaching styles: Behavior of controlling teachers. *Journal of Educational Psychology, 74,* 852-859.

Deci, E.L., Ryan, R.M., and Williams, G.C. (1996). Need satisfaction and the self-regulation of learning. *Learning and Individual Differences, 8,* 165-183.

Deci, E.L., Koestner, R., and Ryan, R.M. (1999). A meta-analytic review of experiments examining the effects of extrinsic rewards on intrinsic motivation. *Psychological Bulletin, 12*(6), 627-668.

Dee, T.S., and Jacob, B.A. (2007). Do high school exit exams influence educational attainment or labor market performance? In A. Gamoran (Ed.), *Will No Child Left Behind Help Close the Poverty Gap?* Washington, DC: Brookings Institution Press.

Dee, T.S., and Jacob, B.A. (2011). The impact of No Child Left Behind on student achievement. *Journal of Policy Analysis and Management, 30*(3), 418-446.

Dixit, A. (2002). Incentives and organizations in the public sector. *Journal of Human Resources, 37,* 696-727.

Doran, H.C., and Cohen, J. (2005). The confounding effect of linking bias on gains estimated from value-added models. In R. Lissitz (Ed.), *Value-Added Models in Education: Theory and Applications.* Maple Grove, MN: JAM Press.

Elmore, R.F. (2004). The problem of stakes in performance-based accountability systems. In S.H. Fuhrman and R.F. Elmore (Eds.), *Redesigning Accountability Systems for Education.* New York: Teachers College Press.

Fehr, E., and Falk, A. (2002). Psychological foundations of incentives. *European Economic Review, 46,* 687-724.

Feuer, M.J. (2008). Future directions for educational accountability: Notes for a political economy of measurement. In K.E. Ryan and L.A. Shepard (Eds.), *The Future of Test-Based Educational Accountability.* New York: Routledge.

Figlio, D.N., and Getzler, L. (2006). Accountability, ability, and disability: Gaming the system? In T.J. Gronberg and D.W. Jansen (Eds.), *Improving School Accountability: Advances in Applied Microeconomics, Volume 14.* Bingley, UK: Emerald Group.

Figlio, D.N., and Kenny, L.W. (2007). Individual teacher incentives and student performance. *Journal of Public Economics, 91*(5-6), 901-914.

Figlio, D.N., and Loeb, S. (2010). School accountability. In E.A. Hanushek and S.J. Machin (Eds.), *Handbook of the Economics of Education, Volume 3.* Amsterdam: North-Holland.

Figlio, D.N., and Winicki, J.F. (2005). Food for thought? The effects of school accountability plans on school nutrition. *Journal of Public Economics, 89*(2-3), 381-394.

Finn, J.D., and Achilles, C.M. (1999). Tennessee's class size study: Findings, implications, and misconceptions. *Educational Evaluation and Policy Analysis, 21*(2), 97-109.

Firestone, W.A. (1985). The study of loose coupling: Problems, progress, and prospects. In A. Kerckhoff (Ed.), *Research in Sociology of Education and Socialization* (vol. 5, pp. 3-30). Greenwich, CT: JAI Press.

Flink, C., Boggiano, A.K., and Barrett, M. (1990). Controlling teaching strategies: Undermining children's self-determination and performance. *Journal of Personality and Social Psychology, 59,* 916-924.

Fredericksen, N. (1994). *The Influence of Minimum Competency Tests on Teaching and Learning.* Princeton, NJ: Educational Testing Service.

Frey, B.S., and Jegen, R.. (2001). Motivation crowding theory: A survey of empirical evidence. *Journal of Economic Surveys, 15,* 589-611.

Fryer, R.G. (2010). *Financial Incentives and Student Achievement: Evidence from Randomized Trials.* Working Paper 15898. Cambridge, MA: National Bureau of Economic Research.

Fuhrman, S.H. (2004). Introduction. In S.H. Fuhrman and R.F. Elmore (Eds.), *Redesigning Accountability Systems for Education.* New York: Teachers College Press.

Fuller, B., Gesicki, K., Kang, E., and Wright, J. (2006). *Is the No Child Left Behind Act Working? The Reliability of How States Track Achievement.* Policy Analysis for California Education. Berkeley: University of California.

Glazerman, S., and Seifullah, A. (2010). *An Evaluation of the Teacher Advancement Program (TAP) in Chicago: Year Two Impact Report.* Washington, DC: Mathematica Policy Research.

Glazerman, S., McKie, A., and Carey, N. (2009). *An Evaluation of the Teacher Advancement Program (TAP) in Chicago: Year-One Impact Report.* Washington, DC: Mathematica Policy Research.

Glewwe, P., Ilias, N., and Kremer, M. (2010). Teacher incentives. *American Economic Journal: Applied Economics, 2*(3), 205-227.

Gonzales, P., Williams, T., Jocelyn, L., Roey, S., Kastberg, D., and Brenwald, S. (2008). *Highlights from TIMSS 2007: Mathematics and Science Achievement of U.S. Fourth- and Eighth-Grade Students in an International Context.* NCES 2009-001, revised. Washington, DC: National Center for Education Statistics, U.S. Department of Education.

Griffin, R.W. (1991). Effects of work redesign on perceptions, attitudes, and behaviors: A long-term investigation. *Academy of Management Journal, 34*(2), 425-435.

Grodsky, E., Warren, J.R., and Kalogrides, D. (2009). State high school exit examinations and NAEP long-term trends in reading and mathematics, 1971-2004. *Educational Policy, 23*(4), 589-614.

Grolnick, W.S. (2003). *The Psychology of Parental Control: How Well-Meant Parenting Backfires.* Mahwah, NJ: Lawrence Erlbaum Associates.

Grolnick, W.S. (2009). The role of parents in facilitating autonomous self-regulation for education. *Theory and Research in Education, 7,* 164-173.

Grolnick, W.S., and Ryan, R.M. (1987). Autonomy in children's learning: An experimental and individual difference investigation. *Journal of Personality and Social Psychology, 52,* 890-898.

Grolnick, W.S., Ryan, R.M., and Deci, E.L. (1991). The inner resources for school achievement: Motivational mediators of children's perceptions of their parents. *Journal of Educational Psychology, 83,* 508-517.

Grolnick, W.S., Gurland, S.T., Jacob, K.F., and Decourcey, W. (2002). The development of self-determination in middle childhood and adolescence. In A. Wigfield and J.S. Eccles (Eds.), *Development of Achievement Motivation* (pp. 147-171). San Diego, CA: Academic Press.

Haertel, E.H., and Herman, J.L. (2005). A historical perspective on validity arguments for accountability testing. In J.L. Herman and E.H. Haertel (Eds.), *Uses and Misuses of Data for Educational Accountability and Improvement* (pp. 1-34, 104th Yearbook of the National Society for the Study of Education, Part 2). Malden, MA: Blackwell.

Hamilton, L.S., Stecher, B.M., Marsh, J.A., McCombs, J.S., Robyn, A., Russell, J.L., Naftel, S., and Barney, H. (2007). *Standards-Based Accountability Under No Child Left Behind: Experiences of Teachers and Administrators in Three States.* Santa Monica, CA: RAND.

Hanushek, E.A., and Raymond, M.E. (2005). Does school accountability lead to improved student performance? *Journal of Policy Analysis and Management, 24*(2), 297-327.

Hanushek, E.A., and Woessmann, L. (2008). The role of cognitive skills in economic development. *Journal of Economic Literature, 46*(3), 607-668.

Harackiewicz, J.M., Abrahams, S., and Wageman, R. (1987). Performance evaluation and intrinsic motivation: The effects of evaluative focus, rewards, and achievement orientation. *Journal of Personality and Social Psychology, 53,* 1,014-1,023.

Heinrich, C.J. (2003). Measuring public sector performance and effectiveness. In G. Peters and J. Pierre (Eds.), *Handbook of Public Administration* (pp. 25-37). London: Sage.

Heinrich, C.J., and Marschke, G.R. (2010). Incentives and their dynamics in public sector performance management systems. *Journal of Policy Analysis and Management, 29*(1), 183-208.

Henderlong, J., and Lepper, M.R. (2002). The effects of praise on children's intrinsic motivation: A review and synthesis. *Psychological Bulletin, 128,* 774-795.

Hightower, A.M. (2010). State of the states: Holding all states to high standards. *Quality Counts 2010. Education Week* (January 14). Available: http://www.edweek.org/ew/articles/2010/01/14/17stateofstates.h29.html?intc=ml [December 2010].

Hill, C.J., Bloom, H.W., Black, A.R., and Lipsey, M.W. (2008). Empirical benchmarks for interpreting effect sizes in research. *Child Development Perspectives, 2*(3), 172-177.

Hill, P., Roza, M., and Harvey, J. (2008). *Facing the Future: Financing Productive Schools.* Center on Reinventing Public Education, University of Washington, Bothell. Available: http://www.crpe.org/cs/crpe/download/csr_files/pub_sfrp_finalrep_nov08.pdf [February 2009].

Ho, A.D., and Haertel, E.H. (2006). *Metric-Free Measures of Test Score Trends and Gaps with Policy-Relevant Examples.* CSE Technical Report 665. Los Angeles: Center for the Study of Evaluation, University of California.

Holme, J.J., Richards, M.P., Jimerson, J.B., and Cohen, R.W. (2010). Assessing the effects of high school exit examinations. *Review of Educational Research, 80*(4), 476-526.

Ingersoll, R.M. (2003). *Who Controls Teachers' Work?* Cambridge, MA: Harvard University Press.

Jackson, K.C. (2010). A little now for a lot later: A look at a Texas advanced placement incentive program. *Journal of Human Resources, 45*(3), 591-639.

Jacob, B.A. (2001). Getting tough? The impact of high school graduation exams. *Educational Evaluation and Policy Analysis, 23,* 99-121.

Jacob, B.A. (2005). Accountability, incentives, and behavior: The impact of high-stakes testing in the Chicago public schools. *Journal of Public Economics, 89*(5-6), 761-796.

Jacob, B.A. (2007). *Test-Based Accountability and Student Achievement: An Investigation of Differential Performance on NAEP and State Assessments.* NBER Working Paper 12817. Cambridge, MA: National Bureau of Economic Research.

Jacob, B.A., and Lefgren, L. (2009). The effect of grade retention on high school completion. *American Economic Journal: Applied Economics, 1*(3), 33-58.

Jacob, B.A., and Levitt, S.D. (2003). Rotten apples: An investigation of the prevalence and predictors of teacher cheating. *Quarterly Journal of Economics, 118*(3), 843-877.

Jaeger, R.M., Cole, J., Irwin, D.M., and Pratto, D.J. (1980). *An Interactive Structure Judgment Process for Setting Passing Scores on Competency Tests Applied to the North Carolina High School Competency Tests in Reading and Mathematics.* Greensboro: University of North Carolina, Center for Education Research and Evaluation.

Kahn, C.M., Silva, E.C.D., and Ziliak, J.P. (2001). Performance-based wages in tax collection: The Brazilian tax collection reform and its effects. *The Economic Journal, 111*(468), 188-205.

Kane, T.J., and Staiger, D.O. (2002). Volatility in school test scores: Implications for test-based accountability systems. In D. Ravitch (Ed.), *Brookings Papers on Education Policy.* Washington, DC: Brookings Institution Press.

Kemple, J.J. (2011). Children First and student outcomes: 2003-2010. In J. O'Day, C. Bitter, and L. Gomez (Eds.), *Education Reform in New York City: Ambitious Change in the Nation's Most Complex School System.* Cambridge, MA: Harvard Education Press.

Klein, S., Hamilton, L., McCaffrey, D., and Stecher, B. (2000). What do test scores in Texas tell us? *Educational Policy Analysis Archives, 8*(49). Available: http://epaa.asu.edu/ojs/article/view/440/563 [May 2011]

Koestner, R., Ryan, R.M., Bernieri, F., and Holt, K. (1984). Setting limits on children's behavior: The differential effects of controlling versus informational styles on intrinsic motivation and creativity. *Journal of Personality, 52,* 233-248.

Koretz, D. (2002). Limitations in the use of achievement tests as measures of educators' productivity. *The Journal of Human Resources, 37*(4), 752-777.

Koretz, D. (2008a). Further steps toward the development of an accountability-oriented science of measurement. In K.E. Ryan and L.A. Shepard (Eds.), *The Future of Test-Based Educational Accountability* (pp. 71-91). Mahwah, NJ: Lawrence Erlbaum Associates.

Koretz, D. (2008b). *Measuring Up: What Educational Testing Really Tells Us.* Cambridge, MA: Harvard University Press.

Koretz, D., and Barron, S.I. (1998). *The Validity of Gains on the Kentucky Instructional Results Information System (KIRIS).* MR-1014-EDU. Santa Monica, CA: RAND.

Koretz, D., and Béguin, A. (2010). Self-monitoring assessments for educational accountability systems. *Measurement, 8,* 92-109.

Koretz, D., and Hamilton, L.S. (2006). Testing for accountability in K-12. In R.L. Brennan (Ed.), *Educational Measurement* (4th ed., pp. 531-578). Westport, CT: American Council on Education/Praeger.

Koretz, D., Linn, R.L., Dunbar, S.B., and Shepard, L.A. (1991). *The Effects of High-Stakes Testing: Preliminary Evidence About Generalization Across Tests.* Paper presented at the annual meetings of the American Educational Research Association and the National Council on Measurement in Education.

Koretz, D., Barron, S., Mitchell, K., and Stecher, B. (1996a). *The Perceived Effects of the Kentucky Instructional Results Information System (KIRIS).* MR-279-PCT/FF. Santa Monica, CA: RAND.

Koretz, D., Mitchell, K., Barron, S., and Keith, S. (1996b). *The Perceived Effects of the Maryland School Performance Assessment Program.* CSE Technical Report No. 409. Los Angeles: Center for the Study of Evaluation, University of California.

Kremer, M., Miguel, E., and Thorton, R. (2009). Incentives to learn. *Review of Economics and Statistics, (91)*3, 437-456.

Ladd, H.F., and Lauen, D.L. (2009). *Status Versus Growth: The Distributional Effects of School Accountability Policies.* CALDER Working Paper 21. Washington, DC: Urban Institute Press.

Lang, K. (2010). Measurement matters: Perspectives on education policy from an economist and school board member. *Journal of Economic Perspectives, 24*(3), 167-182.

Lavy, V. (2002). Evaluating the effect of teachers' group performance incentives on pupil achievement. *Journal of Political Economy, 110*(6), 1,286-1,317.

Lavy, V. (2009). Performance pay and teachers' effort, productivity, and grading ethics. *American Economic Review, 99*(5), 1,979-2,011.

Lazear, E. (2000). Performance pay and productivity. *American Economic Review, 90,* 1,346-1,361.

Lazear, E. (2006). Speeding, terrorism, and teaching to the test. *Quarterly Journal of Economics, 121*(3), 1,029-1,061.

Lee, J. (1998). State policy correlates of the achievement gap among racial and social groups. *Studies in Educational Evaluation, 24,* 137-152.

Lee, J. (2006). *Tracking Achievement Gaps and Assessing the Impact of NCLB on the Gaps: An In-Depth Look into National and State Reading and Math Outcome Trends.* Cambridge, MA: The Civil Rights Project at Harvard University.

Lee, J. (2008). Is test-driven external accountability effective? Synthesizing the evidence from cross-state causal-comparative and correlational studies. *Review of Educational Research, 78*(3), 608-644.

Lepper, M.R., and Greene, D. (Eds.) (1978). *The Hidden Costs of Reward*. Hillsdale, NJ: Lawrence Erlbaum Associates.

Lepper, M.R., Greene, D., and Nisbett, R.E. (1973). Undermining children's intrinsic interest with extrinsic rewards: A test of the "overjustification" hypothesis. *Journal of Personality and Social Psychology, 28*, 129-137.

Linn, R.L. (2000). Assessment and accountability. *Educational Researcher, 29*(2), 4-16.

Linn, R.L. (2003). Performance standards: Utility for different uses of assessments. *Education Policy Analysis Archives, 11*(31). Available: http://epaa.asu.edu/epaa/v11n31/ [May 2011].

Linn, R.L. (2007). *Considerations When Selecting and Combining Measures*. Paper presented at a workshop at the National Academies, November 16, Washington, DC.

Linn, R.L. (2008). Educational accountability systems. In K.E. Ryan and L.A. Shepard (Eds.), *The Future of Test Based Accountability*. New York: Routledge.

Linn, R.L., and Dunbar, S.B. (1990). The nation's report card goes home: Good news and bad about trends in achievement. *Phi Delta Kappan, 72*(2), 127-133.

Locke, E.A., and Latham, G.P. (2002). Building a practically useful theory of goal setting and task motivation. *American Psychologist, 47*(9), 705-717.

Martorel, F. (2004). *Do High School Graduation Exams Matter? A Regression Discontinuity Approach*. Draft paper. Berkeley: Department of Economics, University of California.

McDonnell, L. (2008). The politics of educational accountability: Can the clock be turned back? In K.E. Ryan and L.A. Shepard (Eds.), *The Future of Test-Based Accountability*. New York: Routledge.

McLaughlin, D., Bandeira de Mello, V., Blankenship, C., Chaney, K., Esra, P., Hikawa, H., Rojas, D., William, P., and Wollman, M. (2008). *Comparison Between NAEP and State Mathematics Assessment Results: 2003*. Washington DC: National Center for Education Statistics.

Meyer, J.W., and Rowan, B. (1977). Institutionalized organizations: Formal structure as myth and ceremony. *American Journal of Sociology, 83*, 340-363.

Meyer, J.W., and Rowan, B. (1978). The structure of educational organizations. In M.W. Meyer (Ed.), *Environments and Organizations* (pp. 78-109). San Francisco: Jossey-Bass.

Michaelides, M.P., and Haertel, E.H. (2004). *Sampling of Common Items: An Unrecognized Source of Error in Test Equating*. Technical Report. Los Angeles: Center for the Study of Evaluation and National Center for Research on Evaluation, Standards, and Student Testing.

Muralidharan, K., and Sundararaman, V. (2011). Teacher performance pay: experimental evidence from India. *Journal of Political Economy, 119*(1), 39-77.

National Commission on Excellence in Education. (1983). *A Nation at Risk: The Imperative for Educational Reform*. Washington, DC: U.S. Department of Education.

National Research Council. (1996). *Improving America's Schools: The Role of Incentives*. Board on Science, Technology, and Economic Policy, E.A. Hanushek and D.W. Jorgenson, Eds. Washington, DC: National Academy Press.

National Research Council. (1997). *Educating One and All: Students with Disabilities and Standards-Based Reform*. Committee on Goals 2000 and the Inclusion of Students with Disabilities, L.M. McDonnell, M.J. McLaughlin, and P. Morison, Eds. Commission on Behavioral and Social Sciences and Education. Washington, DC: National Academy Press.

National Research Council. (1999). *High Stakes: Testing for Tracking, Promotion, and Graduation.* Committee on Appropriate Test Use, J.P. Heubert and R.M. Hauser, Eds. Commission on Behavioral and Social Sciences and Education. Washington, DC: National Academy Press.

National Research Council (2006a). *America's Lab Report: Investigations in High School Science.* Committee on High School Science Laboratories: Role and Vision, S.R. Singer, M.L. Hilton, and H.A. Schweingruber, Eds. Board on Science Education. Division of Behavioral and Social Sciences and Education. Washington, DC: The National Academies Press.

National Research Council. (2006b). *Systems for State Science Assessment.* Committee on Test Design for K-12 Science Achievement. M.R. Wilson and M.W. Bertenthal, Eds. Division of Behavioral and Social Sciences and Education. Washington, DC: The National Academies Press.

National Research Council and Institute of Medicine (2004). *Engaging Schools: Fostering High School Students' Motivation to Learn.* Committee on Increasing High School Students' Engagement and Motivation to Learn. Board on Children, Youth, and Families, Division of Behavioral and Social Sciences and Education. Washington, DC: The National Academies Press.

National Research Council and National Academy of Education. (2010). *Getting Value out of Value-Added: Report of a Workshop.* Committee on Value-Added Methodology for Instructional Improvement, Program Evaluation, and Educational Accountability, H. Braun, N. Chudowsky, and J. Koenig, Eds. Washington, DC: The National Academies Press.

National Research Council and National Academy of Education. (2011). *High School Dropout, Graduation, and Completion Rates: Better Data, Better Measures, Better Decisions.* Committee for Improved Measurement of High School Dropout and Completion Rates, R.M. Hauser and J.A. Koenig, Eds. Washington, DC: The National Academies Press.

Neal, D., and Schanzenbach, D.W. (2010). Left behind by design: Proficiency counts and test-based accountability. *Review of Economics and Statistics, 92*(2), 263-283.

O'Day, J. (2004). Complexity, accountability, and school improvement. In S.H. Fuhrman and R.F. Elmore (Eds.), *Redesigning Accountability Systems for Education.* New York: Teachers College Press.

Papay, J.P., Murnane, R.J., and Willett, J.B. (2010). The consequences of high school exit examinations for low-performing urban students: Evidence from Massachusetts. *Educational Evaluation and Policy Analysis, 32*(1), 5-23.

Pittman, T.S., Davey, M.E., Alafat, K.A., Wetherill, K.V., and Kramer, N.A. (1980). Informational versus controlling verbal rewards. *Personality and Social Psychology Bulletin, 6,* 228-233.

Podgursky, M.J., and Springer, M.G. (2006). *Teacher Performance Pay: A Review.* Working Paper 2006-01. Nashville, TN: National Center on Performance Incentives.

Popham, W.J. (2000). *Modern Educational Measurement.* Needham, MA: Allyn and Bacon.

Prendergast, C. (1999). The provision of incentives in firms. *Journal of Economic Literature, 37,* 7-63.

Rabin, M. (1998). Psychology and economics. *Journal of Economic Literature, 36,* 11-46.

Raudenbush, S.W. (2004). *Schooling, Statistics and Poverty: Can We Measure School Improvement?* The Ninth Annual William H. Angoff Memorial Lecture. Princeton, NJ: Educational Testing Service.

Reardon, S.F., Arshan, N., Atteberry, A., and Kurlaender, M. (2010). Effects of failing a high school exit exam on course-taking, achievement, persistence, and graduation. *Educational Evaluation and Policy Analysis, 32*(4), 498-520.

Reback, R. (2008). Teaching to the rating: School accountability and the distribution of student achievement. *Journal of Public Economics, 92*(5-6), 1,394-1,415.

Richards, C., and Sheu, T. (1992). The South Carolina School Incentive Reward Program: A policy analysis. *Economics of Education Review, 11*(1), 71-86.

Rothstein, R. (2008). *Holding Accountability to Account: How Scholarship and Experience in Other Fields Inform Exploration of Performance Incentives in Education.* National Center on Performance Incentives, Working Paper 2008-04. Available: http://www.eric.ed.gov/ERICWebPortal/search/detailmini.jsp?_nfpb=true&_&ERICExtSearch_SearchValue_0=ED510530&ERICExtSearch_SearchType_0=no&accno=ED510530 [December 2010].

Rouse, C.E., Hannaway, J., Goldhaber, D., and Figlio, D. (2007). *Feeling the Florida Heat? How Low-Performing Schools Respond to Voucher and Accountability Pressure.* CALDER Working Paper 13. Washington, DC: Urban Institute Press.

Rowan, B., and Miskel, C.G. (1999). Institutional theory and the study of educational organizations. In J. Murphy and K.S. Louis (Eds.), *Handbook of Research on Educational Administration.* San Francisco, CA: Jossey-Bass.

Rummel, A., and Feinberg, R. (1988). Cognitive evaluation theory: A meta-analytic review of the literature. *Social Behavior and Personality, 16,* 147-164.

Ryan, R.M. (1982). Control and information in the intrapersonal sphere: An extension of cognitive evaluation theory. *Journal of Personality and Social Psychology, 43,* 450-461.

Ryan, R.M., and Brown, K.W. (2005). Legislating competence: The motivational impact of high-stakes testing as an educational reform. In A. Elliot and C. Dweck (Eds.), *Handbook of Competence and Motivation.* New York: Guilford Press.

Ryan, R.M., and Grolnick, W.S. (1986). Origins and pawns in the classroom: Self-report and projective assessments of individual differences in children's perceptions. *Journal of Personality and Social Psychology, 50,* 550-558.

Sallaz, J. (2009). *The Labor of Luck: Casino Capitalism in the United States and South Africa.* Berkeley: University of California Press.

Shapira, Z. (1976). Expectancy determinants of intrinsically motivated behavior. *Journal of Personality and Social Psychology, 34*(65), 1,235-1,244.

Shepard, L.A. (1993). Implications for standard setting of the National Academy of Education evaluation of the National Assessment of Educational Progress achievement levels. In *Proceedings of the Joint Conference on Standard Setting for Large-Scale Assessments* (vol. II, pp. 143-160). Washington DC: National Assessment Governing Board and National Center for Education Statistics.

Shepard, L.A. (2003). Reconsidering large-scale assessment to heighten its relevance to learning. In J.M. Atkin and J.E. Coffey (Eds.), *Everyday Assessment in the Science Classroom.* Arlington, VA: National Science Teachers Association.

Shepard, L.A. (2008). A brief history of accountability testing. 1965-2007. In K.E. Ryan and L.A. Shepard (Eds.), *The Future of Test-Based Educational Accountability.* New York: Routledge.

Smith, M.S., and O'Day, J. (1990). Systemic school reform. *Journal of Education Policy, 5*(5), 233-267.

Springer, M.G., and Winters, M.A. (2009). *New York City's School-Wide Bonus Pay Program: Early Evidence from a Randomized Trial.* Working Paper 2009-02. Nashville, TN: National Center on Performance Initiatives.

Springer, M.G., Ballou, D., and Peng, X. (2008). *Impact of the Teacher Advancement Program on Student Test Score Gains: Findings from an Independent Appraisal.* Working Paper 2008-19. Nashville, TN: National Center on Performance Incentives.

Springer, M.G., Ballou, D., Hamilton, L., Le, V.-N., Lockwood, J.R., McCaffrey, D.F., Pepper, M., and Stecher, B.M. (2010). *Teacher Pay for Performance: Experimental Evidence from the Project on Incentives in Teaching.* Nashville, TN: National Center on Performance Initiatives.

Staiger, D.O., and Rockoff, J.E. (2010). Searching for effective teachers with imperfect information. *Journal of Economic Perspectives, 24*(3), 97-118.

Stecher, B.M. (2002). Consequences of large-scale, high-stakes testing on school and classroom practice. In L.S. Hamilton, B.M. Stecher, and S.P. Klein (Eds.), *Making Sense of Test-Based Accountability in Education*. Santa Monica, CA: RAND.

Stecher, B.M., Bohrnstedt, G.W., Kirst, M., McRobbie, J., and Williams, T. (2001). Class-size reduction in California: A story of hope, promise, and unintended consequences. *Phi Delta Kappan, 82*(9), 670-674.

Stevens, M.L. (2007). *Creating a Class: College Admissions and the Education of Elites*. Cambridge, MA: Harvard University Press.

Stulich, S.E., Eisner, E., and McCrary, J. (2007). *National Assessment of Title I Final Report, Volume I: Implementation*. NCEE 2008-4012. Institute of Education Sciences, National Center for Education Evaluation and Regional Assistance. Washington DC: U.S. Department of Education.

Tang, S.-H., and Hall, V.C. (1995). The overjustification effect: A meta-analysis. *Applied Cognitive Psychology, 9*, 365-404.

Vallerand, R.J., Fortier, M.S., and Guay, F. (1997). Self-determination and persistence in a real-life setting: Toward a motivational model of high-school dropouts. *Journal of Personality and Social Psychology, 72*, 1,161-1,176.

Warren, J.R., Jenkins, K.N., and Kulick, R.B. (2006). High school exit examinations and state-level completion and GED rates, 1975 through 2002. *Educational Evaluation and Policy Analysis, 28*(2), 131-152.

Weick, K. (1976). Educational organizations as loosely coupled systems. *Administrative Science Quarterly, 21*, 1-19.

White, K.W., and Rosenbaum, J.E. (2008). Inside the black box of accountability: How high-stakes accountability alters school culture and the classification and treatment of students and teachers. In A.R. Sadovnik, J.A. O'Day, G.W. Bohrnstedt, and K.M. Borman (Eds.), *No Child Left Behind and the Reduction of the Achievement Gap: Sociological Perspectives on Federal Education Policy*. New York: Routledge.

Wiersma, U.J. (1992). The effects of extrinsic rewards in intrinsic motivation: A meta-analysis. *Journal of Occupational and Organizational Psychology, 65*, 101-114.

Wong, M., Cook, T.D., and Steiner, P.M. (2009). *No Child Left Behind: An Interim Evaluation of Its Effects on Learning Using Two Interrupted Time Series Each with Its Own Non-Equivalent Comparison Series*. Working Paper WP-09-11. Evanston, IL: Institute for Policy Research, Northwestern University.

Appendix

Biographical Sketches of
Committee Members and Staff

MICHAEL HOUT (*Chair*) earned a B.A. in history and sociology from the University of Pittsburgh and M.A. and Ph.D. degrees in sociology from Indiana University. He taught at the University of Arizona for 8 years before moving to Berkeley in 1985. He teaches courses on inequality and data analysis. In his research, Dr. Hout uses demographic methods to study social change in inequality, religion, and politics. He and Claude Fischer recently published *Century of Difference* (Russell Sage Foundation, 2006), a book on social and cultural trends in the United States during the 20th century that exemplifies this approach. Another book, *The Truth about Conservative Christians* with Andrew Greeley (University of Chicago Press, 2006) also takes this approach. A couple of illustrative papers include "Tightening Up: Declining Class Mobility During Russia's Market Transition" (*American Sociological Review*, October 2004), "The Demographic Imperative in Religious Change" (*American Journal of Sociology*, September 2001) and "How 4 Million Irish Immigrants Came to be 40 Million Irish Americans" (with Josh Goldstein, *American Sociological Review*, April 1994). Previous books are *Following in Father's Footsteps: Social Mobility in Ireland* (Harvard University Press 1989) and, with five Berkeley colleagues, *Inequality by Design* (Princeton University Press, 1996). Dr. Hout's honors include the Clogg Award from the Population Association of America in 1997, election to the American Academy of Arts and Sciences in 1997, the National Academy of Sciences in 2003, and the American Philosophical Society in 2006. Mike is the Natalie Cohen chair of sociology and demography at the Berkeley Population Center. He previously served on the National Research Council Committee for the Redesign of the U.S. Naturalization Tests.

DAN ARIELY is the James B. Duke professor of psychology and behavioral economics at Duke University. Previously, he was the Alfred P. Sloan professor of behavioral Economics at the Massachusetts Institute of Technology. He holds a joint appointment among the Fuqua School of Business, the Center for Cognitive Neuroscience, the School of Medicine, and the Department of Economics—all at Duke University. Dr. Ariely is a social scientist who is interested in issues of rationality, irrationality, decision making, behavioral economics, and consumer welfare. Projects include examinations of online auction behaviors, personal health monitoring, the effects of different pricing mechanisms, and the development of systems to overcome day-to-day irrationality. He has a Ph.D. in business administration from Duke University, as well as a Ph.D. in cognitive psychology from the University of North Carolina at Chapel Hill.

GEORGE P. BAKER is the Herman C. Krannert professor of business administration (on leave) at the Harvard Business School. He has published works on management incentives, leveraged buyouts, organizational economics, and the relationship between a firm's ownership structure and its management. Dr. Baker's work focuses on the problem of managerial performance measurement, and its role in the design of incentive systems and on the structure and performance of organizations. He is also the author of the book *The New Financial Capitalists: Kohlberg, Kravis, Roberts and the Creation of Corporate Value* (Cambridge University Press, 1998). For the past 2 years, Baker has been on leave from the Harvard Business School, serving as the vice president of community wind at the Island Institute, a Rockland, Maine-based nonprofit. He has been the driving force behind the Fox Islands Wind Power project in Vinalhaven Maine, and serves as the chief executive officer of Fox Islands Wind, LLC. He has also worked with numerous other communities to explore and develop community wind on the Maine coast. He serves on the Maine Governor's Task Force on Ocean Energy, and is a member of the advisory board of Neptune Wind, an offshore wind development company. At Harvard Business School, Baker teaches in the MBA program, as well as in the doctoral program. Prior to joining the faculty at Harvard, he worked both as a consultant with Temple, Barker and Sloane, and as a marketing manager with Teradyne, Inc. Baker holds a Ph.D. in business economics from Harvard University and an MBA from the Harvard Business School.

HENRY BRAUN is Boisi professor of education and public policy at Boston College. Until 2007, he held the position of distinguished presidential appointee at the Educational Testing Service, where he served as vice president for research management from 1990 to 1999. Dr. Braun has published in the areas of mathematical statistics and stochastic modeling, the analysis of large-scale assessment data, test design, expert systems, and assessment technology. His current interests include the interplay of testing and education policy. He has investigated such issues as the structure of the black-white achievement gap, the relationship between state education policies and state education outputs, and the effectiveness of charter schools. Dr. Braun is a co-winner of the Palmer O. Johnson Award from the American Educational Research Association (1986), and a co-winner of the National Council for Measurement in Education award for Outstanding Technical Contributions to the Field of Educational Measurement (1999). He has a Ph.D. in mathematical statistics from Stanford University.

ANTHONY S. BRYK is the ninth president of the Carnegie Foundation for the Advancement of Teaching. He held the Spencer Chair in Organizational Studies in the School of Education and the Graduate School of Business at Stanford University from 2004 until assuming Carnegie's presidency in September 2008. Prior to Stanford, he held the Marshall Field IV Professor of Education post in the sociology department at the University of Chicago, where he founded the Center for Urban School Improvement which supports reform efforts in the Chicago Public Schools. Bryk also founded the Consortium on Chicago School Research, which has produced a range of studies to advance and assess urban school reform. In addition, he has made contributions to the development of new statistical methods in educational research. At Carnegie, he is leading work on strengthening the research and development infrastructure for improving teaching and learning. Dr. Bryk holds a B.S. from Boston College, an Ed.D. from Harvard University, and in 2010, was conferred an honorary doctorate by Boston College for his contributions to education reform.

EDWARD L. DECI is professor of psychology, Gowen professor in the social sciences, and codirector of the Human Motivation Program at the University of Rochester. For 40 years, Dr. Deci has been engaged in a program of research on human motivation, much of it in collaboration with Richard M. Ryan, that has led to and been organized by Self-Determination Theory. He has published ten books, including *Intrinsic Motivation* (1975); *The Psychology of Self-Determination* (1980); *Intrinsic Motivation and Self-Determination in Human Behavior* (coauthored with R.M. Ryan, 1985); and *Why We Do What We Do* (1995). His writings have been translated into seven languages, including Japanese, German, and Spanish. He is a grantee of the National Institute of Mental Health, the

National Institute of Child Health and Human Development, the National Science Foundation, the Institute of Education Sciences, and a fellow of the American Psychological Association and the American Psychological Society. Dr. Deci has lectured and consulted for corporations, public school systems, mental health agencies, universities, and governmental bureaus throughout twenty-four countries on six continents. He holds a Ph.D. in psychology from Carnegie Mellon University and was an interdisciplinary post doc at Stanford University. Dr. Deci has a private practice in psychotherapy and for 12 years was chairman of the board of the Institute for Research and Reform in Education.

CHRISTOPHER F. EDLEY, Jr., is dean and professor of law at the University of California at Berkeley School of Law and faculty codirector of the Chief Justice Earl Warren Institute on Race, Ethnicity and Diversity, a multidisciplinary think tank. Previously, he was a professor at Harvard Law School, where he was founding codirector of the Harvard Civil Rights Project. His areas of special interest are administrative law, education policy, and race. His public service includes a 6-year term as a member of the U.S. Commission on Civil Rights, an assistant director of the White House domestic policy staff during the Carter Administration, and associate director of the Office of Management and Budget during the Clinton Administration. He served as a special counsel to President Clinton and as a senior adviser on the President's race initiative. He has also served on a national nonpartisan commission created to conduct an independent review of the No Child Left Behind (NCLB) Act. He is a trustee of the Russell Sage Foundation and of the Century Foundation, and a fellow of the National Academy of Public Administration, the Council of Foreign Relations, the American Law Institute, and the American Academy of Arts and Sciences. He received a B.A. in mathematics and economics from Swarthmore College and a J.D. and a master of public policy degree from Harvard's Law School and JFK School of Government, respectively.

STUART W. ELLIOTT (*Study Director*) has directed the Board on Testing and Assessment of the National Research Council (NRC) since 2003. His work at the NRC includes a variety of projects related to educational assessment, accountability, standards, teacher qualifications, skill demands, and information technology. He is also a partner of a small firm specializing in postal and environmental analyses. Previously, Dr. Elliott was an economic consultant for several private-sector consulting firms, a research fellow in cognitive psychology and economics at Carnegie Mellon University, and a visiting scholar at the Russell Sage Foundation. He has a Ph.D. in economics from the Massachusetts Institute of Technology.

GENO FLORES is chief deputy superintendent of public instruction for the California Department of Education. He previously served as executive director of school improvement for the Los Angeles Unified School District, as chief academic officer for Prince George's County Public Schools in Maryland, and as deputy superintendent of the San Diego City Schools. Prior to that, he served as the deputy superintendent of assessment and accountability for the California State Department of Education, and in a similar capacity for the Long Beach Unified School District, where he led the district's High School Reform Program. A lifelong teacher and learner, Mr. Flores has more than 29 years of experience in education, 20 of those years as a teacher and coach. He served as a project director for the Center for Research on Evaluations, Standards, and Student Testing (CRESST) at the University of California, Los Angeles, on the development of assessments for the National Board for Professional Teaching Standards. He has served on numerous advisory boards at both the state and national level and on the National Research Council's Committee on the Use of School Level Assessment Data. He has a masters in education, teaching and learning from Stanford University.

CAROLYN J. HEINRICH is the director of the La Follette School of Public Affairs, professor of public affairs and affiliated professor of economics, and a Regina Loughlin Scholar at the University of Wisconsin–Madison. As of August 2011, she will be the Sid Richardson professor of public affairs, an affiliated professor of economics and the director of the Center for Health and Social Policy at the Lyndon B. Johnson School of Public Affairs at the University of Texas at Austin. Her research focuses on social welfare and education policy, public management and performance management, and social-program evaluation. She frequently works directly in her research with governments at all levels, including with the federal government on evaluations of workforce development programs, with states on their social welfare and child support programs, school districts in the evaluation of supplemental educational services and other educational interventions, and governments such as Brazil and South Africa on their poverty reduction and human capital development programs. In 2004, Dr. Heinrich received the David N. Kershaw award for distinguished contributions to the field of public policy analysis and management by a person under age 40. Prior to her appointment at the University of Wisconsin–Madison in 2003, Dr. Heinrich was an assistant professor at the University of North Carolina at Chapel Hill and held an academic research appointment at the University of Chicago. She received her Ph.D. in public policy studies from the University of Chicago.

PAUL HILL is a professor at the University of Washington Bothell and director of the Center on Reinventing Public Education. The Center, which is funded by foundations and businesses, studies alternative governance and financing systems for public elementary and secondary education. He is a nonresident senior fellow of the Brookings and Hoover Institutions. Before joining the University of Washington faculty, Paul Hill worked as a senior social scientist at RAND. For most of that time, his research focused on the reform of elementary and secondary education. He conducted studies of site-based management, governance of decentralized school systems, effective high schools, business-led education reforms, and immigrant education. Dr. Hill directed the National Institute of Education's Compensatory Education Study (a congressionally-mandated assessment of federal aid to elementary and secondary education) and conducted research on housing and education for the Office of Economic Opportunity. He also served 2 years as a congressional fellow and congressional staff member. He has a Ph.D. in political science from Ohio State University.

THOMAS J. KANE is professor of education and economics at the Harvard Graduate School of Education; faculty director of the Center for Education Policy Research, a program that partners with states and districts to evaluate innovative policies; and deputy director for research and data in the Education Program of the Bill & Melinda Gates Foundation. His work has investigated a range of education policies: test score volatility and the design of school accountability systems, teacher recruitment and retention, financial aid for college, race-conscious college admissions and the economic payoff of a community college education. Recently, he has directed the Measures of Effective Teaching project at the Gates Foundation. From 1995 to 1996, Kane served as the senior staff economist for labor, education, and welfare policy issues within President Clinton's Council of Economic Advisers. From 1991 through 2000, he was a faculty member at the Kennedy School of Government. Kane has also been a professor of public policy at the University of California, Los Angeles, and has held visiting fellowships at the Brookings Institution and the Hoover Institution at Stanford University.

DANIEL M. KORETZ is a professor of education at Harvard University. Previously, he was a professor of educational research, measurement, and evaluation at Boston College and a senior social scientist at RAND Education in Washington, DC. His research is primarily on educational assessment, particularly as a tool of education policy. A primary emphasis in his work has been the effects of high-stakes testing, including effects on schooling and the validity of score gains. His research has included studies of the effects of testing programs, the assessment of students with disabilities, international differences in the variability of student achievement, the application of value-added models to educational achievement, and the development of methods for validating scores under high-stakes conditions. His current work focuses on the design and evaluation of test-focused educational accountability systems. Dr. Koretz founded and chairs the International Project for the Study of Educational Accountability, an international network of scholars investigating improved approaches to educational accountability. Dr. Koretz is a member of the National Academy of Education. His doctorate is in developmental psychology from Cornell University. Before obtaining his degree, Dr. Koretz taught emotionally disturbed students in public elementary and junior high schools.

KEVIN LANG is a professor of economics at Boston University. An elected fellow of the Society of Labor Economists, he is also a research associate of the National Bureau of Economic Research (NBER) and of the Center for Research and Analysis of Migration (University College, London), a research fellow of the Institute for the Study of Labor (Bonn), a fellow of the Center for the Study of Poverty and Inequality (Stanford University), and has for many years been a member of the advisory board of the Canadian Employment Research Forum. He is a coeditor of *Labour Economics*, the journal of the European Association of Labor Economists. Before joining Boston University, he spent a year at NBER as an Olin Foundation fellow and prior to that was an assistant professor at the University of California, Irvine. During his tenure at Boston University, he has twice held appointments at the Massachusetts Institute of Technology for a year, once as a visiting scholar and once as a visiting professor and has been a visiting scholar at the Collegio Carlo Alberto, the University of New South Wales, and the Center for Research and Analysis of Migration. He spent 3 months at the New Zealand Institute of Economic Research on a Fullbright Fellowship, and he was the recipient of a Sloan Foundation Faculty Research Fellowship. He is the author of *Poverty and Discrimination* (Princeton University Press) and has published widely in leading academic journals. Dr. Lang is currently a member of the National Research Council's Board on Testing and Assessment. He holds a Ph.D. in economics from the Massachusetts Institute of Technology, an M.Sc.

in economics from the University of Montreal, and a BA in philosophy, politics and economics (PPE) from Oxford University. For 13 years, he was an elected member of the school board in Brookline, Massachusetts.

SUSANNA LOEB is a professor of education at Stanford University, faculty director of the Center for Education Policy Analysis and a codirector of Policy Analysis for California Education (PACE). She specializes in the economics of education and the relationship between schools and federal, state and local policies. Her research addresses teacher policy, looking specifically at how teachers' preferences affect the distribution of teaching quality across schools, how pre-service coursework requirements affect the quality of teacher candidates, and how reforms affect teachers' career decisions. She also studies school leadership and school finance, for example looking at how the structure of state finance systems affects the level and distribution of resources across schools. Dr. Loeb is a senior fellow at the Stanford Institute for Economic Policy Research, a faculty research fellow at the National Bureau of Economic Research, a member of the policy council of the Association for Policy Analysis and Management, coeditor of *Educational Evaluation and Policy Analysis*, and past president of the Association of Education Finance and Policy.

MICHAEL LOVAGLIA is professor and director of the Center for the Study of Group Processes in the Department of Sociology at the University of Iowa. He is also a faculty affiliate of the university's Institute for Inequality Studies. His interests include social psychology, especially power and status processes, the reciprocal effects of evolution and physiology on social behavior, social factors that affect academic performance, theory construction, and the sociology of science. Current research projects involve power in exchange networks, group process effects on IQ scores, the effects of emotions on status processes, and explaining why more women than men now attend colleges and universities. A new project, Best Schools for Athletes, investigates how schools can promote athletic and academic excellence without compromising either goal. He has a Ph.D. in sociology from Stanford University.

LORRIE A. SHEPARD is dean of the school of education and distinguished rofessor at the University of Colorado at Boulder. Her research focuses on psychometrics and the use and misuse of tests in educational settings. Technical topics include validity theory, standard setting, and statistical models for detecting test bias. Her studies evaluating test use include identification of learning disabilities, readiness screening for kindergarten, grade retention, teacher testing, effects of high-stakes testing, and classroom assessment. She is a past president of the American Educational Research Association and past president of the National Council on Measurement in Education. She was elected to the National Academy of Education (NAEd) in 1992 and is immediate past resident of NAEd. Dr. Shepard served on the National Research Council's (NRC) Board on Testing and Assessment as well as several NRC committees, including the Committee on Assessment in Support of Instruction and Learning. She has been editor of the *Journal of Educational Measurement* and the *American Educational Research Journal* and interim editor of *Educational Researcher*. She has received career awards from the National Council on Measurement in Education and from the American Educational Research Association.

BRIAN STECHER is a senior social scientist and the associate director of RAND Education. Stecher's research focuses on measuring educational quality and evaluating education reforms, with a particular emphasis on assessment and accountability systems. During his 20 years at RAND, he has directed prominent national and state evaluations of No Child Left Behind, Mathematics and Science Systemic Reforms, and Class Size Reduction. He produced two recent reports exploring the use of performance-based accountability, *Organizational Improvement and Accountability: Lessons for Education from Other Sectors*, and *Toward a Culture of Consequences: Performance-Based Accountability Systems for Public Services*. Dr. Stecher has served on expert panels relating to standards, assessments, and accountability for the National Academies, and is currently a member of the Board on Testing and Assessment. He has published widely in professional journals, and he is currently a member of the editorial board of *Educational Assessment*. He received his Ph.D. from the University of California, Los Angeles.